WORDS OF LIFE

THE BIBLE DAY BY DAY
WITH THE SALVATION ARMY

PENTECOST EDITION
MAY-AUGUST 2000

Hodder & Stoughton

LONDON SYDNEY AUCKLAND

AND THE SALVATION ARMY

British Library Cataloguing in Publication Data
A record for this book is available from the British Library

ISBN 0 340 72201 0

Typeset by Avon Dataset Ltd, Bidford-on-Avon, Warks

Printed and bound in Great Britain by
Caledonian International

Hodder and Stoughton Ltd
A Division of Hodder Headline
338 Euston Road
London NW1 3BH

Contents

'One Step at a Time'

Abbreviations used for Bible Versions

AV	Authorised (King James) Version
GNB	Good News Bible
JB	Jerusalem Bible
JBP	J.B. Phillips – The New Testament in Modern English, 1972 Edition
JM	James Moffatt Bible
LB	Living Bible-Kenneth Taylor
NASB	New American Standard Bible
NEB	New English Bible
NIV	New International Version
NKJV	New King James Version
NRSV	New Revised Standard Version
RAV	Revised Authorised Version
REB	Revised English Bible
RSV	Revised Standard Version

Words of Life is a Bible-based daily devotional book. It moves through the Scriptures systematically, always with the goal of enriching the spiritual life of its users. The NIV is our chosen translation; the choice being based on the fact that it is the most used translation. Readers who prefer another translation should accept, with pleasure, the added insights their preferred version affords. On those occasions when we move steadily through a passage of Scripture, sampling its truths in leisurely fashion, another version could be used with profit.

Other Abbreviations:

SASB	*The Song Book of The Salvation Army*, 1986
H&H	*Happiness and Harmony* – a supplementary song and chorus book (Salvationist Publishing & Supplies, Ltd.)
WoL	*Words of Life*

All unattributed verse is by the author, Harry Read.

The Father of Compassion
2 Corinthians 1:1–7

'Praise be to the God and Father of our Lord Jesus Christ, the Father of compassion and the God of all comfort' (v. 3, NIV).

In this letter, which we know as the Second Letter to the Corinthians, the apostle's opening words (*vv. 1–3*) follow closely his introduction to some of his other letters (*cf. 1 Cor 1:1–3; Gal 1:1–5; Eph 1:1,2*). Having considered these statements earlier in our meditations on his First Letter to the Corinthians (*WoL 14–20 Aug 98*), we will not dwell on them here except to stress their importance. Paul was careful to present himself as an apostle 'by the will of God' (*v. 1*). He was determined also to make it clear that the church was 'the church of God' (*v. 2*). No human hand made the Church and the Church was accountable therefore, not to apostles or elders, but to God himself.

We note too the blessing of grace and peace which is given in the name of 'God our Father and the Lord Jesus Christ' (*v. 2*). The name of Lord, 'the name that is above every name' (*Phil 2:9b*), equals the Old Testament 'Jehovah' and, as such, confirms Christ's divinity. Jesus was our Lord's birth name and emphasises his humanity; the name Christ (Greek – *Christos*) means the 'Anointed One' or the Messiah, and this witnesses to his role in our redemption.

God is the 'Father of compassion' (*v. 3b*). Because of their circumstances, the Corinthians may have doubted God's compassion just as it is easy to doubt it today. This, of course, is one of the reasons why Jesus came to earth. By our own efforts we cannot 'fathom the mysteries of God' (*Job 11:7*) but Jesus came to show us the Father. The works of Jesus the Son are the works of God the Father (*John 14:8–11*). The compassion of Jesus points to the compassion of the Father. The nature of the Son is the nature of the Father. We have just cause to praise.

PRAYER
The more of Christ I see,
The more his love I feel,
The more is God to me,
And his compassions real.
Through Christ, I know God's heart of love,
And, following Christ, God's love I prove.

A Personal Experience
2 Corinthians 1:1–7

'The Father of tender mercies and the God of all comfort, who comforts me in all my distress' (vv. 3b, 4a, JM).

'Comfort' is a great biblical word. Presumably the word appears often in Scripture because our frailty requires that we be reassured and strengthened so frequently. It is significant that the Greek word which is translated 'comfort' in the New Testament shares the same root as the name for the Holy Spirit, who is so often known as the Comforter (*John 14:16 AV*). As we would expect, the Holy Spirit is much more than a Comforter, but he is that, and he fulfils the role wonderfully well.

The Greek word means 'calling to one's side' and it is the Holy Spirit in all his power, and with all his resources, who draws alongside us. He comes to strengthen us, help us to handle our problems and stresses. Not only does the Scripture inform us and the history of God's people confirm it, but our hearts tell us that the God and Father of our Lord Jesus Christ must be the God of all comfort. It is one thing, however, to know this well-attested truth, but another thing to validate it in our own experience. This validation is possible and essential because Christianity is a faith which is built upon relationships: the relationship of Jesus with the Father and our relationship with the Father through Jesus (*John 17:20–26*).

James Moffatt's translation of our key verse is helpful to us because he moved from the statement that the Father is the 'God of all comfort' to the personal affirmation, 'who comforts me in all my distress'. Sooner or later the pressures of life require that we stand firm when others crumble or would, at least, be perplexed or resentful. The reason for our strength and stability is the fact that the comfort which God alone can give is available to us, and we have learned how to draw on him as our prime resource. He 'comforts *me* in all *my* distress'.

PRAYER
> *Less than thyself will not suffice*
> *My comfort to restore;*
> *More than thyself I cannot have,*
> *And thou canst give no more.*

(*Augustus Montague Toplady, SASB 565*)

The Ministry of Comfort

2 Corinthians 1:1–7

'God ... who comforts us in all our troubles, so that we can comfort those in any trouble with the comfort we ourselves have received from God' (vv. 3b, 4, NIV).

Who can better comfort another than the person who has been comforted? Those people who have walked the dark, lonely road of grief and learned that through the Holy Spirit, Christ has been a comforting companion on the way, are well qualified to give support. Credibility is a vital element in helping others. We listen to those who have experienced suffering and sorrow; the people who 'do understand' because they are familiar with the doubts, darkness, pain and, wonderfully, the comfort of God.

Paul was writing out of deep personal experience as he shared with the Corinthians (*vv. 8–10*); indeed, certain members of the Corinthian church were responsible for some of his troubles. Even so, Paul had the mindset which enabled him to turn difficulties into opportunities and blessings, and he knew that he was qualified to comfort other people because he himself had been comforted. He recognised this as an important ministry both for himself, and others, to exercise.

The value of bringing comfort and encouragement to other people is being proved daily. Many churches, for example, have initiated support groups for people with specific needs, and many groups that have no Christian base have similar aims. If, however, such groups are not able to point to the 'God of all comfort' their influence must be limited.

When we belong to Christ, we belong to God and we belong to each other. This special relationship means that comfort and encouragement are lovely ministries that we can, and should, fulfil. To comfort is to strengthen. Our ministry will not, therefore, be superficial: we will know that through us also the Lord is coming alongside one of his needy people.

PRAYER

> Make me a channel of your peace,
> Where there's despair in life, let me bring hope;
> Where there is darkness, only light;
> And where there's sadness, even joy.

(based on a prayer of *St Francis of Assisi*)

The Troubled Heart

2 Corinthians 1:3–11

'[God] comforts us in all our troubles' (v. 4a, NIV).

Our troubles are not necessarily the same as those of other people but, whatever the cause of our difficulties may be, the comfort we receive from the Father is sufficient. The meaning of the word 'trouble' is pressure (*cf. v. 8b*), a word much used today. If our workload is heavy, we feel pressure; if money is scarce, relationships become tense, illness threatens, loneliness intensifies or failure comes again, we feel pressure.

Although Paul was in conflict with the Corinthians he was referring, not to their intransigence, but to difficulties which were his lot as an ambassador of Christ. As he remarked, 'We were under great pressure, far beyond our ability to endure, so that we despaired even of life' (*v. 8b*). We are left to imagine the nature of those troubles but, since Paul tended to take difficulties in his stride (*cf. Acts 16:25*), they must have been serious. Because Christ was central to his life, Paul had no difficulty in identifying his discipleship as the reason for his troubles. He was convinced that, in a profoundly spiritual sense, the sufferings of Christ were flowing over him (*v. 5a*) but, as following Christ was the reason for his hardships, so he was convinced that Christ was the source of his comfort (*v. 5b*).

The apostle did not, however, intend the Corinthians to assume that every difficulty came directly from the hand of the Master. As we know to our cost, many of our difficulties are self-generated; even so, the solutions are found in him. He is our deliverer (*v. 10*): his comfort is the source of our endurance – and what a blessing that is! Every church has within its membership saintly people who demonstrate an ability to endure with patience and cheerfulness difficulties of such magnitude that we catch our breath as we consider them. Almost always, these saints make light of their sufferings and ascribe their ability to endure to the grace of God. He never fails us.

PRAYER

Show me, O Master, how I can endure,
And how with courage I can face distress.
Grant to me patience, Lord, and cheerfulness,
The faith I need to be in you secure.
Then let me, Lord, my comfort widely share,
That more may know your healing love and care.

One Thing after Another
2 Corinthians 1:12–17

'Now this is our boast: Our conscience testifies that we have conducted ourselves in the world, and especially in our relations with you, in the holiness and sincerity that are from God' (v. 12a, NIV).

Having founded the Corinthian church, Paul was their father in Christ (*cf. 1 Cor 3:10; 4:15*) and, as such, could have expected expressions of love and high regard from them. Instead, as both the first and second letters to the church indicate, Paul was often misunderstood and maligned. The group in the church which was most highly critical of him seemed to go from one extreme to another in their attempts to devalue his ministry.

In the brief passage of Scripture chosen for today, we find that exception was taken to a change Paul had made in his plans to visit them (*vv. 15–17*). They should have known that his love for them would guarantee that any change in plan must have been born of purest motives. Paul's critics, however, were ungenerous and they attacked him by claiming that he was a man who spoke as the world spoke, saying 'Yes' when he meant 'No' (*v. 17*). The charge, untrue and mean-spirited, led Paul to boast that he and his companions had conducted themselves in a manner consistent with a godly sincerity (*v. 12b*). It was a bold claim to make.

We are used to people boasting about their achievements, but Paul was boasting about qualities which had come from God. Once, when he boasted of himself, he was ill at ease and apologetic, although he believed that he had to make the boast (*11: 16–21*). Even so, he made it clear that he would 'boast of the things that show my weakness' (*11:30*).

The truth Paul was affirming to the Corinthians and which, after these many years, his words affirm today, is that God enables us to live in our present difficult circumstances in a spirit of true holiness. We do not need to compromise God's standards – he will make us equal to our task.

PRAYER

> *Jesus, confirm my heart's desire*
> *To work and speak and think for thee;*
> *Still let me guard the holy fire,*
> *And still stir up thy gift in me.*

(*Charles Wesley, SASB 199*)

A Spirited Defence

2 Corinthians 1:15–24

'But as surely as God is faithful, our message to you is not "Yes" and "No" ' (v. 18, NIV).

Paul never separated his theology from everyday life; in fact, what he believed about God determined everything he did and said. Because he knew that God was the source of all goodness (*cf. Rom 11:33–36*) he assumed that godliness should be revealed in him. Since God was the source of integrity, he, Paul, would reflect that quality in his own life.

Because Paul had changed his plans and had not visited the Corinthians as previously intended, his detractors had accused him of wilful deception. They bracketed Paul with the people of the world who said 'Yes' when they meant 'No'. It was an unjust charge that the apostle was at pains to refute. He replied by affirming that his original plans had been thoughtfully and responsibly made (*v. 17a*), and the Corinthians ought to have known that a man as trustworthy and dedicated as he would not have changed those plans without due cause. Had they entertained a doubt they should have given him the benefit of it and not have presumed that he would have acted in a devious or careless way.

Without audacity or irreverence Paul made the remarkable claim that as God is faithful, so is he. As God's 'Yes' is reliable so is his and, as God's promises are sure, so are his. The claim was both bold and true, and it was true because Paul was standing firm in Christ (*v. 21a*). Was it generosity of spirit that made Paul say that the Corinthians, including his unkind critics, were also standing firm in Christ? Or was he indicating that it is possible to be in Christ and still reveal weaknesses of spirit? Commentators occasionally remind us that 'we are to become what we are' – a memorable phrase which means that the work of grace done within us is far greater than we understand, and that the gap between the Spirit's actual work in us and our attitudes and behaviour needs to be closed. The disciple's integrity should be closer to the integrity of God.

PRAYER

Your Holy Spirit dwells within
Exerting boundless energy
To make an end of all my sin,
And make it clear Christ lives in me;
Now, Lord, my doubting mind persuade
That Christ in me can be displayed.

Homesickness

Luke 15:11–21 (following 9.4.2000)

'I will set out and go back to my father and say to him: Father, I have sinned against heaven and against you' (v. 18, NIV).

We continue with an earlier Sunday's thought of the prodigal coming 'to his senses' and deciding to return to the home he should never have left in the first place. Trying to visualise the prodigal son's dismay, disillusionment and self–disgust which led to repentance, Helmut Thielicke wrote, 'In the last analysis it is not merely disgust, it is above all homesickness.' This definition strikes important chords within us, as Will Lamartine Thompson's gospel hymn suggests (*SASB 264*):

> *Come home, come home!*
> *Ye who are weary, come home!*
> *Earnestly, tenderly, Jesus is calling,*
> *Calling, O sinner, come home!*

Many of us recall the tranquillity which rolled over us when we repented and returned to the Father: a serenity compounded of relief, contentment and completeness. The rebellion was over – the foolishly affirmed independence was forsaken, the self-will was surrendered and we knew the joy of acceptance. We who had been lost had been found – and it was good to be home.

We ought always to feel at home in the Father's house and with the Father's household (*Eph 2:19*). Here we find love and 'everything we need for life and godliness' (*2 Pet 1:3*). Within this unique community we are given gifts which build us up and build up also the body of Christ (*Eph 4:11–13*). Furthermore, the household of God assures us of our inheritance (*Col 1:12*) and the privilege of sharing the Master's mission.

PRAYER

> *Where else but in the Father's home*
> *Is deep contentment found?*
> *Where else but in his company*
> *Can love and grace abound?*
> *All that we are will harmonise*
> *When all we are God glorifies.*

PRAYER SUBJECT   *Christians who work among the elderly.*

The Centrality of Christ

2 Corinthians 1:15–24

'For the Son of God, Jesus Christ, who was preached among you by me and Silas and Timothy, was not "Yes" and "No", but in him it has always been "Yes" (v. 19, NIV).

There was nothing negative or indecisive about Christ. He knew who he was, knew also his role, powers and mission. He was the most positive man the world has known. His word was always clear and uncompromising, yet appealing to all who had the 'ears to hear' his message.

Paul's sensitivity towards the Holy Spirit meant that when he touched a subject it began to yield truth beyond normal imaginings. He perceived, for instance, that Jesus was not only positive and clear in his speech so that his 'Yes' and 'No' were unmistakable, but that Jesus was God's 'Yes' to all his promises (*v. 20*). The scope of these promises is wider than the Messianic promises, wonderful as those promises are. We can almost feel the heavenly excitement when Christ became incarnate, and almost hear the heavenly host shouting 'Yes' at his birth. They knew that the manger scene had been planned before the world was founded and, we allow ourselves to imagine, rejoiced accordingly.

Jesus was the 'Yes' regarding the love of a Father-God. He was the 'Yes' that God was the great Deliverer (*Exod 3:1ff.*), the great Shepherd of Israel (*Ezek 34:11–16*) who would send his Spirit to indwell his people (*Joel 2:28*). More even than that – Jesus was the 'Yes' that God had entered into our world to fulfil his plans for every believer.

The existence of other faiths can trouble some Christians today, but Paul's word is as inspired now as it was when he was writing to the Corinthians: Jesus is the 'Yes' to all that God is and plans to do in our world. He was more than one of the prophets, or the founder of another religion, or merely a gifted and good man: he is the 'Yes' of God; the only Son of God (*John 3:16*), the 'Saviour of the world' (*John 4:42*).

PRAYER

> *Our Lord is all the proof God gives*
> *To this dark world that he is real,*
> *And that within our world he lives*
> *To save our souls – our wounds to heal.*
> *Our Lord is all the proof our hearts should need,*
> *In him, God's promises are guaranteed.*

The Reason Why
2 Corinthians 2:1–4

'So I made up my mind that I would not make another painful visit to you' (v. 1, NIV).

Paul had promised the Corinthians he would visit them, suggesting that he might stay with them for some time (*1 Cor 16:5,6*). In order to resolve the problems in the church he had made a flying visit. This visit proved to be so painful and fruitless that he wrote them his 'severe letter' (*v. 4*) – a letter which has been lost (*WoL 15 Aug 98*) – and decided not to make the promised visit simply because of the pain it would cause them and himself (*vv. 1,2*). Perhaps we ought not to be surprised that the 'severe letter' – written in love out of a near-breaking heart – was used by the Holy Spirit to achieve the desired end. Severe letters if written out of a censorious, judgmental heart do not achieve much good, but letters which are truthful, loving and written in the Spirit of the Lord, must be letters the Holy Spirit can use. In defending himself further against some of his critics, Paul wrote the letter we know as the Second Letter to the Corinthians.

How good it is that Paul chose to bare his heart to his people! Even in a conflict situation, he was able to communicate his love and his overwhelming desire to build them up in the faith. We can see how the tenderness of Paul's love for his people allowed him to affirm the uncompromising principles of the gospel and to do so creatively.

Responsible leadership and discipleship are never without cost. Christian leaders often face difficult people, some of whom are most unwilling to accept counsel; and disciples who are not leaders occasionally find themselves in conflict situations also. It is the way of the Master, who told his disciples, 'A student is not above his teacher, nor a servant above his master . . . If the head of the house has been called Beelzebub, how much more the members of his household!' (*Matt 10:24,25*). Of course, leadership and discipleship have great rewards in this life and in eternity. If we share Christ's sufferings we will share his glory (*cf. 2 Tim 2:12*).

PRAISE

> *To us who share thy pain,*
> *Thy joy shall soon be given,*
> *And we shall in thy glory reign,*
> *For thou art now in heaven.*

(*Charles Wesley*)

The Right Way

2 Corinthians 2:5–11

'I urge you, therefore, to reaffirm your love for him' (v. 8, NIV).

Because this is a letter which Paul would never expect to become a part of Scripture, he did not try to clarify the precise nature of the problem or identify the wrongdoer. Perhaps that is as well. He makes it clear, however, that the offender was led to sorrow and repentance by the congregation (*v. 6*). This result was the major achievement of the 'severe letter' (*v. 4*). In fact, so thorough was the corporate discipline that it appears as though the congregation was prepared to leave the offender in a state of repentance and brokenness without a healing gesture of acceptance.

In Paul's view, although it was wrong to treat a wrongdoer with a tolerance which bordered on tacit approval, it was wrong also to treat a repentant man as though he were a spiritual leper. For this reason he counselled a spirit of forgiveness and acceptance. Perhaps Paul was recalling our Lord's words, 'Forgive us our sins, for we also forgive everyone who sins against us' (*Luke 11:4*). And Paul was not slow to remember how gravely he himself had sinned and how he had been forgiven (*Acts 26:4–18; 1 Tim 1:15*). He knew that if the Church could not forgive or could forgive and not accept, we would all be less than God intended us to be. As one who had been wronged by this now penitent critic, Paul indicated that his own forgiveness of the man was complete (*v. 10*).

We note that Paul's counsel was to 'reaffirm your love for him' (*v. 8*): not making an empty gesture but out of love, presumably the quality of love Christ spoke of in the Upper Room and made possible everywhere (*John 13:34,35*). We assume also that Paul believed that a spirit which leaves people feeling unforgiven and unloved is evil, and is one of the ways in which Satan attempts to outwit the people of God (*v. 11*). How vigilant we must be! It is reasonable and natural to put limitations on our acceptance of one who has offended – but that is not the Master's way.

PRAYER
> Let me, O Lord, forgive like you,
> And love like you, accept like you.
> Give me the wisdom to console
> Each sorrowing, repentant soul.
> Help me to do as you would do,
> Reach out in love as you would do.

Turmoil and Triumph

2 Corinthians 2:12–17

'Now when I went to Troas to preach the gospel ... I still had no peace of mind, because I did not find my brother Titus there' (vv. 12a, 13a, NIV).

Paul took rather a long time to explain why he had not kept his promise to visit the Corinthians (*1:15,16; 1 Cor 16:5*). This was not due to evasiveness but rather because some great truths clamoured for expression, no doubt to the blessing of the Corinthians and, certainly, to the Church ever since. Paul's interruptions included the statement that Christ was the 'Yes' to God's promises (*1:18–22*) and an inspiring exhortation to forgive and restore a penitent member (*vv. 5–11*). Glorious digressions indeed!

Paul had sent Titus to Corinth after the despatch of the 'severe letter' (*v. 4; WoL 15 Aug 98*) and was most anxious about the church there and how the believers would receive Titus. Although God opened doors of opportunity for him in Troas he was so fretful that he could wait no longer for Titus but crossed over to Macedonia to meet him as he returned (*vv. 12,13*). Again Paul interrupted his narrative! He saved the details of his meeting with Titus until later (*7:6–16*), but his joy was immense and, with his heart truly encouraged, he launched into another inspiring digression (*v. 14*).

Scholars tell us that Paul takes his imagery in these verses from the triumphal procession of a general returning to Rome after completing a successful campaign. Clearly, Paul believed that, in spite of conflict and the wounds of battle, those who belong to Christ are guaranteed victory. The reference to fragrance (*vv. 15,16*) recalls the fact that incense was burnt during the procession. To the soldiers of the victorious army it was the fragrance of life, but to the prisoners in the procession who were about to die, it was the fragrance of death. As Paul saw it, Christians are the sweet fragrance of Christ to believers; but to unbelievers Christians and the fragrance of Christ convey a message of judgment. May the lovely fragrance of Christ spread even more widely!

PRAYER
May Jesus mean so much to me,
That others may his likeness see
In all my attitudes and deeds,
In all on which my spirit feeds,
So that wherever I may go
Those near me might his fragrance know.

Letters of Commendation

2 Corinthians 3:1–6

'Are we beginning to commend ourselves again? Or do we need, like some people, letters of recommendation to you or from you?' (v. 1, NIV).

Paul's humility was put to the test by his Corinthian critics. They challenged his authority and he had to defend himself. The apostle felt that he was becoming immodest because of his self-commendation, hence the first question in our key verse. Although he had obtained letters of commendation when he was persecuting Christians (*Acts 9:2*) he carried no such letters with him in his role as pioneer-evangelist. Paul Barnett quotes from H.L. Goudge and makes the apostle's dilemma clear, 'Self-defence is almost impossible without self-commendation. Paul's opponents made the former necessary, and then blamed him for the latter.'

In the absence of letters of commendation the Holy Spirit stimulated Paul to seek for a more valuable endorsement and this he found in the Corinthians themselves. They, the members of the Corinthian church, were the finest letters of commendation or validation it was possible for an evangelist to have. No ordinary testimonial could equal the eloquence of lives won from paganism; of sinners made into saints; of lives brutalised and darkened by the excesses of the world's most evil city being turned into lives which radiated the light of Christ. This letter was written on Paul's heart and anyone could read it (*v. 2*).

More than that, however, they were a letter from Christ to believer and unbeliever alike (*v. 3*). Family, friends, neighbours, enemies – all could look at the new life which shone through their eyes, coloured their speech and changed their lifestyles and read there the eternal gospel. Christians, whether literate or illiterate, slow to speak or gifted communicators are living letters, and with incredible eloquence they commend their Lord and Master. Such letters of commendation, written 'with the Spirit of the living God' (*v. 3*) are the most powerful of all.

PRAYER

Let me, O Lord, your love commend,
Within my heart your gospel write:
Make me a letter by you penned,
That all who read may read aright,
And know that through this living word,
You are the Christ, the living Lord.

An Overflowing Mind

2 Corinthians 3:4–11

'Now if the ministry that brought death, which was engraved in letters on stone, came with glory ... will not the ministry of the Spirit be even more glorious?' (vv. 7a,8, NIV).

The closer we get to Paul the more we value his originality of mind. We visualise the apostle dictating this letter and, as he pauses for his scribe to write a sentence, we imagine his mind racing away developing new ideas. It seems reasonable to assume that when Paul dictated the words 'written not with ink but with the Spirit of the living God, not on tablets of stone but on tablets of human hearts' (*v. 3b*), he triggered thoughts of Moses receiving the law on Sinai, and began to compare the old covenant with the new covenant. It was another glorious interruption.

Steeped as Paul was in the history of God's people he was aware of the glory of the old covenant. That God should intervene in the life of a captive people, free them from their Egyptian masters and make a nation out of them, was a miracle large enough to astonish any reasonable student. The old covenant had shortcomings as Paul well knew, but he knew of its glory also. He knew that the legalism which was part of the law had been replaced by the dispensation of the Spirit who brings life.

We note also how Paul moved from the embarrassment of commending himself to the Corinthians (*v. 1*) to the more secure 'Not that we are competent in ourselves ... but our competence comes from God. He has made us ... ministers of a new covenant' (*vv. 5,6a*). Paul was struggling to express the glory of the new covenant. He could see its glory and his heart was stirred to worship. He was reaching out for words to describe that glory and not finding them because human language cannot express something so divine. Instead he could use only the words 'glory' or 'glorious' and this he did ten times in a span of five verses (*vv. 7–11*). But what are human letters of commendation (*v. 1*) when the Spirit writes in fire upon the heart, and Almighty God shines with an indescribable glory?

PRAYER
> *God of grace and God of glory,*
>   *On thy people pour thy power;*
> *Now fulfil thy Church's story,*
>   *Bring her bud to glorious flower.*

> (*Harry Emerson Fosdick, SASB 577*)

The Homecoming
Luke 15:11–24 (following 7.5.2000)

'I will set out and go back to my father and say to him: Father, I have sinned against heaven and against you' (v. 18, NIV).

The prodigal son knew that he had surrendered his right to his father's favour. He had taken his share of the inheritance and by the manner of his squandering had shamed his father's name. None knew better than the son that the only approach to his father could be as a servant, hence his proposed confession, 'Father, I have sinned against heaven and against you. I am no longer worthy to be called your son; make me like one of your hired men' (*vv. 18b,19*). But love gave the father a different perspective: he was moved by mercy not recriminations, by love's acceptance rather than pride's rejection.

Had not the father searched the distant horizon longing for his son's return and spent restless nights worrying about his young son's safety and well-being? The loving father would have been unable to get him out of his mind during long, lonely days because love of that quality exacts a price the like of which un-love could not even dream. There is something heroic, not maudlin, about parents' love for their wayward child, and the indescribable longing for the prodigal to return. The parable's integrity is enhanced by the revelation of the father's watchfulness and his spontaneous action in rushing out to welcome his son back home (*v. 20b*).

We can only imagine how many times the son had rehearsed his lines as he journeyed home, but those carefully crafted protestations of remorse and entreaty were brushed aside by his father's joy. This was not the time for recriminations or sadness, but for celebration. 'This son of mine was dead and is alive again; he was lost and is found' (*v. 24*).

PRAISE

My son, who once was lost, is found again:
    To me and to my family has returned.
The angels reinforce this glad refrain,
    They know how bright a father's love can burn.
This is a most exhilarating day,
My long-lost son is home, and home to stay.

PRAYER SUBJECT   *Parents with children in the 'distant country'.*

Old and New

2 Corinthians 3:4–11

'He has made us competent as ministers of a new covenant – not of the letter but of the Spirit; for the letter kills, but the Spirit gives life' (v. 6, NIV).

To support his contention that he and his friends did not need human commendation, Paul stated that God had made them competent 'as ministers of a new covenant'. By emphasising the new covenant and contrasting its glory with the glory of the old covenant, Paul leads us to believe that part of the Corinthian problem related to Jewish Christians. These were men who, although part of the Church, depended too much on their heritage and could not see the glory of the work of Christ. Had they known Christ, they would have been more forward-looking.

Speaking for God, the prophet Jeremiah had said, 'The time is coming . . . when I will make a new covenant with the house of Israel . . . It will not be like the covenant I made with their forefathers . . . I will put my law in their minds and write it on their hearts' (*Jer 31:31–33*). In the same vein Ezekiel had said, 'I will give you a new heart and put a new spirit in you; I will remove from you your heart of stone and give you a heart of flesh' (*Ezek 36:26*). Jewish Christians had no valid cause to exalt the old covenant and undermine the validity of the new.

Jesus had spoken of his blood being the 'blood of the [new] covenant, which is poured out for many for the forgiveness of sins' (*Matt 26:28*). The old covenant was sealed by the blood of animal sacrifices but the new covenant was sealed by the blood of Jesus, the Passover lamb sacrificed for us (*1 Cor 5:7*). The old covenant was written on stone but the new covenant is written on the heart. The old covenant could not be kept because the law was impossible to keep, whereas the new covenant is wonderfully possible to keep because of the indwelling Spirit. By his indwelling the Holy Spirit guarantees us adequate resources. The glory of the new covenant must, therefore, outshine the glory of the old covenant.

PRAYER
*I thank you, Lord, for this new covenant
    Which by your love and mercy includes me.
I am so glad that it is relevant,
    And gives my faltering heart security.
You make each day, O Lord, a day of grace,
And where I am you make a holy place.*

A Shrewd Illustration

2 Corinthians 3:12–18

'We are not like Moses, who would put a veil over his face to keep the Israelites from gazing at it while the radiance was fading away' (v. 13, NIV).

From their history Israel had known that, following the reading from the Book of the Covenant to the people, Moses ascended Mount Sinai to be in the presence of God for forty days and forty nights (*Exod 24:1ff.*). When he came down Moses was unaware that the radiance of the Lord shone from his face. The radiance glowed so strongly that, for the benefit of his people, he covered his face with a veil, removing it only when he returned to the presence of the Lord (*Exod 34:29–35*). In time, the glory faded from Moses's face and this fact Paul pressed into service to illustrate the impermanent nature of the glory of the old covenant.

With the same ingenuity, Paul referred to the veil Moses wore at that time, to suggest that a veil hangs over the sacred writings and over the hearts of the people of Israel. So effective was this veil that it served to hide from them the dawn of a new life in Christ Jesus, and only Christ could take the veil away (*vv. 14–16; cf. v. 18*).

Paul's ability to put a profound truth into simple and memorable words proved itself again with 'where the Spirit of the Lord is, there is freedom' (*v. 17b*). How we cherish that truth even though we know we can never exhaust its meaning! Christians can look upon Christ in his glory and, in consequence, the truth becomes clear that they too can become all and more they ever hoped to be through him. We are at liberty to see, at liberty to be, and at liberty to do. Our limitations are not imposed by Christ but rather by the limitations of our own understanding. The Christian faith owes everything to the truth that we enter into a personal experience of the Lord Jesus Christ. We learn from others but we learn also from that encounter with Jesus. As R.H. Strachan wisely said, 'The Christian does not merely accept certainties, but discovers them.'

PRAYER
> *Take from our eyes the veil*
> *That hides you from our sight,*
> *Let not your love and mercy fail*
> *To bring our souls to light.*
> *But let us on your glory gaze,*
> *And know your glory all our days.*

The Transforming Glory

2 Corinthians 3:17,18

'But we all, with unveiled face beholding as in a mirror the glory of the Lord, are being transformed into the same image from glory to glory' (v. 18a, NASB).

Paul had an advantage over most of us insofar as he had once seen the risen Lord in all his glory. For him, there was a literal Damascus Road experience (*Acts 9:1–6*); for most of us, our Damascus Road, although no less real in its own way, took place within our hearts. Are we not numbered among those of whom our Lord said, 'Blessed are those who have not seen and yet have believed' (*John 20:29b*)? When writing to any of the churches, Paul knew he was writing to those who had never seen Jesus; knew also that the number of those who had seen him was shrinking. We share with the vast majority of Christians the privilege of being exposed to the glory of the Lord – the glory that transforms us.

We cannot see Jesus with the naked eye, but we see him as we read of him in the Scripture. It matters little whether our 'mind's eye' picture of him is accurate but, as we listen to his voice in the Scriptures and observe him at work, our hearts find it easy to recognise him. When we pray to him and share fellowship with him we have no problem with his identity. We *see* him because we *know* him. When we are with other Christians and our hearts are sensitive to the Lord's presence, he is exposing us further to his glory. Our absorption with other things makes the process slower than Christ desires, but he works patiently to transform us into his likeness. To be like him is a claim we would never make – we know ourselves too well for that – but the process is taking place.

We tend to become like the people we admire, and today's sub standard role models are making massive problems for society; but those who make Jesus their pattern are gradually becoming more like him. This encourages us to spend more time in prayer, Bible study, worship and service. The more we learn of him the more Christlike we will be.

PRAYER

Have thine own way, Lord, have thine own way;
Hold o'er my being absolute sway;
Fill with thy Spirit till all shall see
Christ only, always, living in me.

(Adelaide A. Pollard, SASB 487)

Combating Discouragement

2 Corinthians 4:1–6

'Therefore, since through God's mercy we have this ministry, we do not lose heart' (v. 1, NIV).

Part of Paul's strength in ministry was the firm belief that God had selected him to fulfil this role. With all his heart he believed that God had chosen him to be an 'apostle to the Gentiles' (*Gal 2:8*); it was a conviction which gave him unlimited powers of endurance, released his heart and mind for the high aims of the gospel and tutored him in dependence on Christ. The apostle considered his calling to be a privilege, accepting it with total enthusiasm. It was through God's mercy that he had this ministry. Because God had called him, he could hardly be discouraged.

Ministry is not something that engages the energies of leaders and other paid servants of the Church only, although that is often assumed. The words our Lord spoke in the Upper Room belong to us all, not merely the 'full-time' minister, 'You did not choose me, but I chose you and appointed you to go and bear fruit' (*John 15:16*). The strategy behind the Church being the body of Christ is that we are all engaged in ministry. For that reason, the Spirit gives his gifts to each of us (*1 Cor 12:11*).

There is much in life and in the Christian ministry to discourage us. Often we serve unappreciative people. Occasionally we are misunderstood and maligned. Sometimes our physical resources are tested to the limit and discouragement takes its toll. Although we may have to modify our way of working to match our strength, and become better stewards of our talents, the truth remains that since we, like Paul, have our ministry through the mercy of God, losing heart is not a valid option. If, at times, there is much to discourage, there is always more to encourage. The Risen Christ is no less risen when difficulties arise, his grace is no less strong, his presence no less real, and his calling no less sure. We can take heart because it is through God's mercy that we have this ministry.

PRAYER
Jesus calls us; by thy mercies,
Saviour may we hear thy call,
Give our hearts to thy obedience,
Serve and love thee best of all.

(Cecil Frances Alexander, SASB 428)

A Strong Defence

2 Corinthians 4:1–6

'Rather, we have renounced secret and shameful ways; we do not use deception, nor do we distort the word of God' (v. 2a, NIV).

In order to damage Paul's ministry, his critics made outrageous charges against him. In the context of Corinth's twisted morality, the charge of 'secret and shameful ways' was a vile accusation to make, and we wonder if his opponents thought they could prove it. Perhaps they thought that if they threw enough mud some of it would besmirch the apostle. Some scholars think that the accusation of deception relates to deviousness insofar as, by working and refusing to take payment from the congregation, he was seeking a way whereby he might unduly influence the people. It is thought also that the charge of distorting the word of God concerned his use of the Old Testament to support the Christian faith.

This latter charge he answered by declaring that 'by setting forth the truth plainly' they were commending themselves to everyone's conscience (*v. 2*). In that verse also we have another reference to commendation: Paul was obviously content to let his life speak for him. With the thought of the veil still in his mind (*3:18*) Paul could not help saying that to his detractors who were unbelievers, the gospel was hidden by a veil – the veil being the result of the work of the 'god of this age' (*v. 4*).

Paul's strength lay in his firm hold on Christ and, without delay, he returned to his Lord. 'For we do not preach ourselves, but Jesus Christ as Lord, and ourselves as your servants for Jesus' sake' (*v. 5*). In this he was doing what he did best, that is, disclaiming any personal rights, affirming Christ as Lord, and portraying himself as a servant. It must be difficult to maintain an attack on a man who is self-effacing and whose life's work is to project his Master. It is even more difficult when that man says, 'God . . . made his light shine in our hearts to give us the light of the knowledge of the glory of God in the face of Jesus Christ' (*v. 6*)!

PRAISE
The world overcoming by limitless grace,
I worship the Lord in the light of his face;
So with him communing, like him I shall grow,
And life everlasting enjoy here below.

(*Charles Coller, SASB 640*)

Power and Weakness

2 Corinthians 4:7–12

'But we have this treasure in jars of clay to show that this all-surpassing power is from God and not from us' (v. 7, NIV).

When Paul was accosted by Jesus on the Damascus Road he saw the 'glory of God in the face of Christ' (v. 6b; Acts 9:1–6). From that moment he needed no further argument to prove to himself that Jesus was the Christ, the Son of God and, from then onwards, the light of that knowledge shone within him as a constant source of illumination and inspiration. It was the treasure to which he refers in our key verse.

We make the assumption that as he contemplated this treasure Paul became increasingly aware of the frailty of human flesh, not least his own. He had not been gifted with a physique that made people aware of his presence. Furthermore, his eloquence on paper was not matched by a voice that commanded immediate attention (10:10). Our acquaintanceship with Paul through his writings makes *us* wish that we had heard him speak but, according to Paul, *they* found him unimpressive.

Nothing could be more ordinary than a jar of clay ['earthen vessel' (AV)] but it was God's will that his treasure should occupy such a humble container. Although Paul must have been amazingly tough (11:23–29), he was aware of his physical weaknesses (12:7–10). Some of us know the frailty of our 'jar of clay' also. But the weaknesses are not all physical. Paul was conscious of pressure, perplexity, of being hounded because of his faith (vv. 8,9), and those frailties belong to the heart and mind rather than the body. In fact, his feelings were so sensitive that he likened them to carrying around in the body 'the death of Jesus' (v. 10).

How wise Paul was to perceive that the imperfections of the body allow the divine glory to shine more strongly through us! Because of this, Paul knew the value of his weakness and even boasted of it (12:10).

PRAISE

> When with thy Spirit's rich treasure
> My earthen vessel is stored,
> Mine is the service of pleasure,
> Thine all the glory, dear Lord.

(*Ruth Tracy, SASB 457*)

The Homecoming

Luke 15:11–24 (following 14.5.2000)

'Let's have a feast and celebrate' (v. 23, NIV).

A father's love – a mother's love also – does not stand on ceremony when the prodigal returns; the emotions are charged with love and gratitude. No checklist is produced of things that must be said or done. The homecoming in our Lord's parable represented repentance, and the new lifestyle was to be lovingly worked out later. Today, as the father made clear, was a time for acceptance and celebration, hence his command, 'Quick! Bring the best robe . . . a ring . . . and sandals . . . Bring the fattened calf and kill it. Let's have a feast and celebrate' (*vv. 22,23*).

Our Lord's parable has such credibility that we find ourselves wondering whether the father had ensured that there would always be a fattened calf available in expectation of the long hoped-for and prayed-for return of the prodigal. The best robe appeared to cover a travel-stained and sin-stained body, the shoes went over unwashed feet as symbols of acceptance. Nothing was allowed to delay the long-awaited celebration.

Does the fact that the fattened calf was available suggest to us that we ought to be more ready to celebrate than we are? Although there may be much to discourage us at times, perhaps there are occasions when we could and should celebrate and fail to do so. What are our faith and conquests over evil if not opportunities to celebrate? Why can we not celebrate a conversion, or someone's restoration, or an acceptance into church membership? Many other causes for celebration exist, of course. The equivalent of the fattened calf could, perhaps should, always be available, and we can be sure of this: if our celebrations are worthy, all heaven will join in them.

PRAYER

> *O teach my heart to celebrate,*
> *More gratitude to generate;*
> *Grant me the love and faith to bring*
> *My joyful praise an offering*
> *To Christ, whose conquest over death and sin*
> *Allows our celebrations to begin.*

PRAYER SUBJECT   *For more joy in our Christian lifestyle.*

Preparation for Life
2 Corinthians 4:13–18

'Therefore we do not lose heart. Though outwardly we are wasting away, yet inwardly we are being renewed day by day' (v. 16, NIV).

In this closing paragraph of the chapter Paul repeats some of the opening words, 'we do not lose heart' (*v. 1*). Having been given his ministry through the mercy of God he knew that he had no just cause for discouragement, 'If God is for us, who can be against us?' (*Rom 8:31b*). Even so, Paul had other reasons for encouragement and confidence, one of them being that God was constantly preparing his people for a much greater life – a much greater glory – than could be experienced on earth.

Most young men who volunteer for military service have a conviction that they will survive. The conviction tends to waver when the moment of battle arrives but, instinctively, the young feel they will live for ever. Paul, however, knew differently. He was old enough to know that age and failing health makes the body more vulnerable and less able to bear the heat and burden of the day (*v. 16a*). But Paul was not being morbid, merely factual, when he observed a purpose in it all. When life on earth is lived in the will of God, it is preparation for a much more wonderful and fulfilling life in the eternal world which awaits us.

Writing to the Colossians, Paul counselled them to 'put on the new nature, which is being constantly renewed in the image of its creator' (*Col 3:10 NEB*). It is encouraging to know that day by day the Holy Spirit is renewing us, shaping us indeed, 'to the likeness of his Son' (*Rom 8:29b*). Paul was convinced that our troubles, bad though they may be, are 'light and momentary', and achieve for us an 'eternal glory that far outweighs them all' (*v. 17*). No experience need be wasted but everything can yield a marvellous harvest in the future. Paul did not lose heart because he knew that what we see and experience is temporary but, when the eternal Christ is in focus, what is unseen is eternal (*v. 18*).

PRAYER

Thou art the bread that satisfies for ever,
The inward health that overcomes disease,
The love that lives through death, subsiding never,
My secret fortress and my soul's release.

(*Catherine Baird, SASB 631*)

Our Way of Life

2 Corinthians 5:1–10

'We live by faith, not by sight' (v. 7, NIV).

Thoughts of the impermanence of life must have loomed large in Paul's mind because he continued the theme into this new chapter. He believed that when his earthly tent [body] had fulfilled its task, an eternal house awaited him (*v. 1*). As we have already stated (*WoL 22 May 2000*) life is a time of preparation: what is to come depends on what has already taken place. Robert Browning's words strike the right note:

> *Grow old along with me!*
> *The best is yet to be,*
> *The last of life, for which the first was made:*
> *Our times are in his hand*
> *Who saith, 'A whole I planned,*
> *Youth shows but half; trust God: see all nor be afraid!'*

There is so much more ahead of us than we can even begin to imagine, and God, in his infinite wisdom, has given us his Holy Spirit 'as a deposit, guaranteeing what is to come' (*v. 5*). Because of this, says Paul, we can be confident and 'we live by faith, not by sight' (*v. 7*). If we believe that life is more than mere existence and that the mysteries of human personality, hope, love and the life of Christ on earth are significant, there is no viable alternative left to us than to live by faith. Although many people live by their lower nature, many others are persuaded that the divine element in life cannot be ignored. These prove that following the highest demands of their hearts is not only satisfying but opens up another world, the world where God reigns supreme. We live by faith – we believe that God is real and we are accountable to him (*v. 10*). We believe that Jesus is the Christ and is our way to God. We believe that our citizenship is in heaven. Faith expects no less.

PRAYER
> *O that with yonder sacred throng*
> *We at his feet may fall,*
> *Join in the everlasting song,*
> *And crown him Lord of all!*

(*Edward Perronet, SASB 56*)

The Fear of the Lord

2 Corinthians 5:11–15

'Since, then, we know what it is to fear the Lord, we try to persuade men' (v. 11a, NIV).

Sometimes we refer to people as being fearless, that is, without fear, when accuracy requires that we describe them as courageous. Fearlessness can relate to a lack of knowledge of the consequences whereas courage usually implies that the dangers are known, the feelings of fear have been dealt with, and courageous actions result. Fear is not all bad. Fear of fire, for example, causes us to be careful how we handle it – the fear engenders respect and that is healthy. The fearlessness of some people borders on recklessness and makes us feel even more fearful.

The fear of the Lord to which Paul refers has within it this element of fear of the consequences of defying God. Judgment is a fact and the apostle knew and declared that each of us will be held accountable for our actions (*v. 10*). W.E. Vine describes it as a 'reverential fear of God [which is] a controlling motive of the life, in matters spiritual and moral, not a mere fear of . . . retribution, but a wholesome dread of displeasing him, a fear which banishes the terror that shrinks from his presence'. This fear of the Lord is a large factor in Paul's evangelism (*v. 11b*). He knows the consequences of disobedience and sin (*Rom 6:23*).

Paul would have agreed with the psalmist, 'The fear of the Lord is the beginning of wisdom' (*Ps 111:10a*); agree, also, that such fear is only the *beginning* of wisdom and should continue through life. Not at any time should we be unconcerned about the consequences of disobedience and our reverence for God should always increase. Our friendship with Jesus (*John 15:13–15*), and God's generosity towards us (*cf. Rom 2:4*), ought not to make us feel casual about God, but even more loving and grateful.

PRAYER

We have not feared thee as we ought,
* Nor bowed beneath thine aweful eye,*
Nor guarded deed and word and thought,
* Remembering that God was nigh.*
Lord, give us faith to know thee near,
And grant the grace of holy fear.

(Thomas Benson Pollock, SASB 466)

Further Compulsion
2 Corinthians 5:11–15

'For Christ's love compels us, because we are convinced that one died for all, and therefore all died' (v. 14, NIV).

At one time Paul had been in the grip of an uncontrollable hatred. He had seen the growth of the Church, observed its enthusiasm, its power to attract his fellow–Jews and believed it was a threat to all Israel. He felt he had to do all he could to destroy this new community before it became too powerful to handle and, fuelled by an evil zeal, he attacked the Church (*Acts 26:9–11*). Paul's encounter with Jesus on the Damascus Road broke the power of evil in his life and love replaced the hatred.

With the vigour and initiative he had once used to oppose Christ and persecute his followers, Paul began to exalt Christ and build his Church. It was reasonable for Paul to acknowledge the compelling force of love in his life. His strong sense of indebtedness to God for his redemption and awareness of his call to be the apostle to the Gentiles (*Gal 2:7,8*) meant that his energies were committed to Christ's cause.

It was our Lord's love that held Paul in its grip. He believed that he had been crucified with Christ and that Christ lived within him. He was convinced that Christ had loved him and given his own life up for him (*Gal 2:20*) with the result that he desired above all that Christ should love through him. Christ's love compelled *him* and the same love is seeking to compel *us*. Paul was sure that when Christ died he paid the penalty for our sins: 'we are convinced that one [Christ] died for all' (*v. 14b*). The death penalty was ours also – and Christ paid it (*Heb 2:9*). The statement, 'and therefore all died' (*v. 14c*) simply but gloriously means that God planned that Christ's death to sin should be our death to sin as well, so that we might be alive in him (*v. 15; Rom 6:11*).

PRAYER

O let thy love my heart constrain,
Thy love for every sinner free;
That every fallen soul of man
May taste the grace that found out me,
That all mankind with me may prove
Thy sovereign, everlasting love!

(*Charles Wesley, SASB 140*)

A New Perspective
2 Corinthians 5:16–21

'So from now on we regard no-one from a worldly point of view. Though we once regarded Christ in this way, we do so no longer' (v. 16, NIV).

Was Paul, we wonder, gently rebuking his detractors for measuring him by purely human standards? Had they looked at him and his work and dismissed him as being of little value? If so, it was the dismissiveness of those who measured life by external rather than spiritual means. Once upon a time, Paul had even measured Christ in the same unfortunate way (*v. 16b*). This is not to say that Paul had met Christ personally – most scholars believe that he first met Jesus on the Damascus Road – but it does mean that Paul refused to accept the reports of the Risen Christ as true. To him, Jesus was a man who made false claims about himself and had paid the ultimate penalty. He was but a man and not the Messiah.

From the moment he met Christ on the Damascus Road, however, and saw the 'glory of God in the face of Christ' (*4:6b*), Paul knew that Jesus could be properly understood only by looking at him from an eternal viewpoint. Too many people today try to interpret Jesus from the human perspective and do not see the unreasonableness of so doing. They admit, indeed they press the point, that Jesus was a good man, but do not realise that if that was all he was, then he was deluded and dishonest. He was either the Messiah or he was an impostor. Bewildering though it may be, Jesus can be properly appraised only in the light of eternity.

In the same way we are to look at each other and all whom we meet. If we assess people in human terms, we will not see the eternal dimension that is part of us all. Jesus died for the best and for the worst of us. All people can be saved (*v. 15*) and, being saved, can be filled with the Holy Spirit. We become heirs of the kingdom and joint heirs with Christ (*cf. Rom 8:12–17*). With a potential of this magnitude Paul was right to say, 'from now on we regard no-one from a worldly point of view' (*v. 16a*).

TO PONDER
> Men die in darkness at your side,
>   Without a hope to cheer the tomb;
> Take up the torch and wave it wide,
>   The torch that lights time's thickest gloom.

(Horatius Bonar, SASB 683)

In Christ

2 Corinthians 5:16–21

'Therefore, if anyone is in Christ, he is a new creation; the old has gone, the new has come!' (v. 17, NIV).

Because Paul had concluded that Jesus could not be measured by ordinary standards (*v. 16*) but had to be recognised as the Christ, he began our key verse with 'Therefore'. From this new evaluation of the Christ proceeded the truth that anyone who was 'in' him was a new creation. Much has been written on the wonder of being in Christ and more will be written in the future because it is deeply satisfying to experience, and its potential is limitless. Suffice it to say at this point, that when we are in Christ we love him; we know that he has redeemed us and, through his Spirit's ministry within us, his resurrection life is ours (*see Eph 1:3–14*). When we are in Christ, we can hardly be other than a new creation.

Although Paul's terminology was different from our Lord's, his thoughts ran on the same lines. Jesus told Nicodemus, 'I tell you the truth, no-one can see the kingdom of God unless he is born again' (*John 3:3*). He knew, and our self-knowledge confirms, that we are far past the point where a little tinkering with our lives can restore us. Nothing less than a new birth is called for, and being in Christ achieves that objective. This unmerited relationship with Jesus is dramatic because in the moment we trust him we find that the old has gone and the new has come.

This transaction of grace explains the changed facial expression, the different attitudes, and the confidence in the future of the new disciple. Obviously, the habits of years occasionally reassert themselves; new disciples can be forgetful of their new status in Christ; there can be a momentary or involuntary lapse, but the truth remains: those who are in Christ are a new creation. A glorious future awaits all who are in Christ.

PRAISE

> Long my imprisoned spirit lay
>   Fast bound in sin and nature's night;
> Thine eye diffused a quickening ray;
>   I woke; the dungeon flamed with light.
> My chains fell off, my heart was free,
> I rose, went forth, and followed thee.

(*Charles Wesley, SASB 283*)

Meanwhile . . .

Luke 15:11–32 (following 21.5.2000)

'The older son was in the field. When he came near the house, he heard music and dancing' (v. 25, NIV).

The parable gives no indication why the father did not send a servant to the older brother who was working in the field to inform him of his brother's return. Perhaps we are to imagine that he might have refused to come or, having come, would spoil the celebration before it had commenced. When the older brother learned from a servant the nature of the celebration, he did refuse to enter the house, and the father went out to him there to plead with him to share in the festivities (*v.28*).

We have some sympathy for the elder brother. He had been loyal to his father and, presumably, as the father aged had taken more responsibility for the property, probably adding to his father's wealth in the process. The older brother had been at hand also when his father needed him, which was much more than could be said of the younger son. But it was the latter whose homecoming had caused the celebrations to commence.

The older brother's resentment is pinpointed in a number of ways, not least when he refers to his brother as 'this son of yours' (*v. 30a*). Gently the father reassured his older son because he, too, was deeply loved, but in replying he referred to the prodigal as, 'this brother of yours' (*v. 32b*). It is a true but sad observation that the older son, although he had never left home or been disobedient, had not become like his father in love. The father loved both of his sons equally, but neither son loved his father enough. The younger son loved so little that he left home, and we know that the older son loved little because he could not rejoice with his father in the prodigal's return.

PRAYER

> *I am praying, blessèd Saviour,*
> *To be more and more like thee;*
> *I am praying that thy Spirit*
> *Like a dove may rest on me.*

(Fanny Crosby, SASB 584)

PRAYER SUBJECT   *Christian Counsellors.*

The Ministry of Reconciliation
2 Corinthians 5:16–21

'All this is from God, who reconciled us to himself through Christ and gave us the ministry of reconciliation' (v. 18, NIV).

In any act of moral and spiritual redemption, the initiative has to come from God. When the people of Israel were oppressed by Pharaoh in Egypt it was God who initiated their rescue (*Exod 3ff.*). Another period of captivity was ended by a sovereign act of God (*Ezra 1:1–4*), and when the time was ripe for the entire world to be redeemed again God acted (*Luke 1:5ff.*). Men and women cannot rescue or redeem themselves.

The gulf between a holy God and an unholy people is enormous. Guilty and sinful though we are, we cannot forgive ourselves. Such forgiveness belongs to God. Neither can we approach God and suggest that he might discuss ways which could lead to reconciliation. He alone can begin such a process – and he has done so. Believers are in Christ – are a new creation with a glorious future because God chose to reconcile us. Our soul-destroying sins have been forgiven; they were dealt with at Calvary (*Col 2:13–15*), and our lives are hidden with Christ in God (*Col 3:3*).

God does not limit his giving to us. Not only are we reconciled but *he gives to us the ministry of reconciliation*. Having been redeemed and brought into his favour, declared to be his children and heirs with Christ (*Rom 8:14–17*), we have been granted the privilege of declaring to other people the joys of reconciliation – and what joys they are! Ours is such a burdened world. Large numbers of people are desperate for fulfilment and their chosen ways of finding it simply produce more difficulties. Others feel the pressure of their inadequacies – they know that life has much more to offer but they have yet to find it. Others need a new start in life, and so on, but *it is we who have this ministry of reconciliation*.

PRAYER

Which of all our friends to save us,
Could or would have shed his blood?
But our Jesus died to have us
Reconciled in him to God;
This was boundless love indeed;
Jesus is a friend in need.

(*John Newton*)

Ambassadors for Christ

2 Corinthians 5:16–21

'We are therefore Christ's ambassadors' (v. 20a, NIV).

Ambassadors, unlike presidents and prime ministers, do not often feature in the world's headlines. As ambassadors they are resident in the country to which they have been appointed and spend their time representing their nation in many ways. Ambassadors conduct themselves in such a way as to commend their own people to the host country: they maintain channels of communication which further economic, cultural and political relationships. Because they speak for their own government, ambassadors are expected to subordinate their own views, speaking and acting in ways which enhance their nation and its values. It is of interest that the embassy is regarded as being part of the ambassador's home country and a serious breakdown in relationships, for whatever cause, can result in the withdrawal of an ambassador.

Much of the forgoing helps us to understand Paul's affirmation to the Corinthians, 'We are therefore Christ's ambassadors.' We are ambassadors for a number of reasons but, in this context, we occupy that role because we are ministers of reconciliation. No better ministry can be exercised than the one God has designed to give peace to the world. No greater privilege can be given to us than being his chosen representative.

As Jesus was sent to our needy world, so we have been sent (*John 17:18*) and, having been chosen and commissioned, we are to live fruitful lives (*John 15:16*). We are a pilgrim people passing from this life to an eternal city (*Phil 3:20*) and are meant to represent our heavenly Father. Paul believed that in appealing to unbelievers he was doing so on God's behalf, 'as though God were making his appeal through us. We implore you, on Christ's behalf: Be reconciled to God' (*v. 20b*). The way God has chosen to make his kingdom known is through his ambassadors; and we who often feel inadequate have been equipped to do this task.

PRAYER
I am unworthy, Lord.
My hands by sin have been defiled;
How can I challenge this our world
Demanding all be reconciled?
But I am called your name to represent,
Your gracious strategy to implement.

God's Chosen Way

2 Corinthians 5:16–21

'God made him who had no sin to be sin for us' (v. 21a, NIV).

In this English translation words of one syllable make our key verse one of the most profound statements of all time. We are reconciled to God because Jesus, who 'had no sin [was made] sin for us'. God is able to do as he pleases, but one of the things he cannot do is to ignore human sin. It is we humans, with our disabled morality, who can say something like, 'why don't we let bygones be bygones and start afresh?' when confession and forgiveness are more appropriate courses to follow. Because God is a holy God he can do no other than take sin seriously.

One of the major reasons behind the Incarnation of our Lord was to handle human sin in the most loving and effective way. It was to be a way which honoured the holiness of God and give to the forgiven sinner a new opportunity to live righteously. Theories about the effectiveness of Calvary have abounded throughout the centuries and Christian scholars in the future will still wrestle with the 'why' and 'how' of it, because Christ's sacrifice for sin – so simple to make part of human experience – is so difficult to express in language. But Paul, in this brief statement, seems to get near to defining the sacrifice, and we know there is more to come.

In a mysterious but gloriously effective way, Jesus, himself sinless, bore the sins of the world as he was crucified. Whatever price had to be paid for our sin Jesus paid it, and we can be reconciled to God. As Isaac Watts wrote so penitently and gratefully (*SASB 120*):

> *My soul looks back to see*
> *The burden thou didst bear*
> *When hanging on the accursèd tree,*
> *And knows her guilt was there.*

Through that same sacrificial act the forgiven soul becomes righteous. Paul Barnett sums it up for us: 'The sinless one takes our sin in himself; the sinful ones are given the "righteousness of God" in exchange.' It is not a fair exchange, but how very glad we are of it!

PRAYER   *Grant me the wisdom, Lord, to see*
                          What I can be through Calvary.

Team Work

2 Corinthians 6:1,2

'As God's fellow-workers we urge you not to receive God's grace in vain' (v. 1, NIV).

For a number of reasons, when we are in Christ we become extraordinary people; one of those reasons being that we become fellow-workers with God. We have become part of the family – God's family – business. It is incredible that we who once were opposed to him should be trusted in this way but that is how the divine forgiveness operates. We are not simply tolerated but are set to work on the project that is closest to the heart of God – namely, the redemption of the world. He can give no greater role to his people than that. Not that we can ever be more than junior partners in his enterprise but that, surely, is enough.

God, of course, takes the major role. It is his Spirit who works in the world, convicting the world of sin, righteousness and judgment (*John 16:8–11*). The same Holy Spirit equips and empowers us for ministry, thereby enabling us to play our part in befriending, encouraging, witnessing, preaching, praying and nurturing. How important it is that we should play our part well! We are fellow-workers by God's choice!

Clearly, one of the roles of a fellow-worker with God is to encourage people to consider seriously their relationship with God: 'we urge you not to receive God's grace in vain' (*v. 1b*). The Corinthians to whom Paul addressed this plea were so persuaded by the argument that salvation is by the law, that they were in serious danger of missing the truth that salvation is an act of sovereign grace. Their error mattered enormously to Paul because if they lost sight of the gospel of grace, they had lost sight of everything worthwhile. Christ had come into the world not simply to give mankind another option: his coming indicated the seriousness of humanity's spiritual condition. It was a matter of the greatest importance, therefore, that his misguided friends should accept the gospel, and Paul, as God's fellow-worker, was playing his part in influencing them.

PRAYER
As fellow-workers, Lord, with you,
* Your chosen witnesses of grace,*
Instruct us so that all we do
* Might help the lost to seek your face.*
Make us, Lord, bold in faith and prayer,
And keen your mercy to declare.

The Day of God's Favour
2 Corinthians 6:1,2

'I tell you, now is the time of God's favour, now is the day of salvation' (v. 2b, NIV).

Paul had good cause to press everyone to choose Christ's way without delay. The pagan way of life with its debauchery, lack of hope and joy was so obviously a way of death (cf. Rom 8:5–8; Eph 4:17–19). It was imperative they should leave paganism behind. On the other hand, the Jew, with his life dominated by legalism and ceremonies which did not touch the heart, stood in great need of this gospel of grace. To pagan and religious groups alike Jesus – with his offer to ordinary people of reconciling love, with the prospect of being infilled by the Holy Spirit and with the gift of the opportunity to live righteously – was the only viable alternative in life. Jesus offered light and life to a dying world – as he does today.

To help him in his appeal to his opponents in Corinth, Paul used a verse from Isaiah in which the Lord promised that Israel would be a 'light for the Gentiles', and that 'in the time of my favour I will answer you, and in the day of salvation I will help you' (Isa 49:6b,8a). The apostle had no doubt: the long-promised day of favour and salvation had arrived and should not – could not – be ignored. The day of favour is the day of deliverance from sin and from the bondage of the law. It is the day of peace, joy, fulfilment – the day when the dreams of the heart are met, when the hopes of immortality find substance in the resurrection of Jesus, and when human personality can blossom to the full.

To Paul, Christ and his gospel were irresistible: on every count the day of favour should be welcomed. Not only does God require it, and that is reason enough for acceptance, but we need it in order to live adequately. It would be wrong to say this is a 'now or never' situation, but experience teaches that we are more ready to decide for Christ at one time than another. A failure to respond now may result in failure to respond at any time. *Now* is so much better than *never* (cf. Heb 3:13).

PRAYER
Your Spirit, Lord, has come with me to stay,
And by him is my longing heart renewed;
The day of favour always is today,
A day of hope, of faith, of plenitude.
Your promises, O Lord, were made in love,
And daily those great promises I prove.

An Essential Link
2 Corinthians 6:3–13

'We put no stumbling-block in anyone's path, so that our ministry will not be discredited' (v. 3, NIV).

In recent years many people have been affirming that what they do in their private lives has no bearing on the work they do in the public arena; as though lack of integrity in one area cannot affect the need for integrity in another. This is a serious position to adopt and one that is potentially very damaging to society. As Christians we have due cause for concern over this attempt to remove personal morality from everyday life. Paul had no doubt, however, that if the leader is discredited the cause must suffer. For this reason he said, 'We put no stumbling-block in anyone's path, so that our ministry will not be discredited', adding further, 'Rather, as servants of God we commend ourselves in every way' (*v. 4*).

Paul believed that the leader must lead in every possible way. He must be more dedicated, honourable and, surely, display more integrity than other people. In their own way, too, the Corinthians believed the same. It was because enemies of Paul had sown seeds of doubt in their minds concerning Paul's fitness to lead that it became necessary for him to defend himself: hence these many statements of self-commendation.

From the important, but largely negative angle, Paul stated that neither he nor his associates had placed stumbling-blocks in the paths of others. Having made that clear, he proceeded to show the very positive ways in which they had proved themselves worthy of acceptance. The list is inspiring and merits careful reading. As a record of the cost of discipleship it is almost breathtaking, ranging as it does from hardship and persecution, through wielding 'weapons of righteousness in the right hand and in the left' (*v. 7*), to 'sorrowful, yet always rejoicing; poor, yet making many rich; having nothing, and yet possessing everything' (*v. 10*). Paul had earned the right to ask them to open their hearts to him (*vv. 11–13*).

PRAYER

> O help me, Master, so to live,
>   That others may be drawn to you;
> I want your Holy Spirit's touch
>   On everything I think and do.
> On you, O Lord, I would depend,
> So that your gospel I commend.

The Everlasting Truth
Luke 15:28–32 (following 28.5.2000)

'We had to celebrate and be glad, because this brother of yours was dead and is alive again; he was lost and is found' (v. 32, NIV).

Of the many suggestions made concerning the role of the older brother, we prefer that one which makes him comfortable with the law but uncomprehending of grace. He knew the importance of duty, obedience, hard work, loyalty and perseverance, but was unable to understand how the father could welcome back a son who had broken all the laws of family relationships. Why should the father, he appeared to reason, reward rebellion and failure in the younger son and not appear to acknowledge, with a similar generosity, the faithfulness of the older son? There is no indication that the father's attempts at reassurance were successful; the older son seemed to remain completely baffled.

How we thank God for his grace! Grace is not only more attractive than the law, it is much more adventurous. What other than divine grace would take risks by giving so much for so little? Grace is also more effective than the law, insofar as it transforms lives and builds up the family of God. Some years later Paul was to say to the Ephesians, 'You were dead in your transgressions and sins . . . but because of his great love for us, God, who is rich in mercy, made us alive with Christ . . . it is by grace you have been saved' (*Eph 2:1–5*). This is a statement which expands the father's explanation, 'this brother of yours was dead and is alive again; he was lost and is found' (*v. 32*).

Some of those who heard Jesus tell this parable would fail to see the older son and his legal rectitude in themselves, but others would take heart. There is always a way back to the Father because he is the 'God of all grace' (*1 Pet 5:10*). Countless other prodigals have taken hope also, having learned from Jesus that the Father will welcome all who are anxious to return.

PRAISE
>Ring the bells of Heaven, there is joy today
>For a soul returning from the wild!
>See, the Father meets him out upon the way,
>Welcoming his weary, wandering child.

(*William Orcutt Cushing, SASB 550*)

A Conflict of Interests
2 Corinthians 6:14–18

'What agreement is there between the temple of God and idols?' (v. 16, NIV).

Our chosen Scripture portion, when considered apart from its immediate context, can cause pain. Paul was *not* saying that where either wife or husband is an unbeliever they should separate from each other. There are many fine Christian men and women who have a good marriage even though their spouse has made no commitment to our Lord. In fact, in his earlier letter, Paul had given good reasons for such couples to stay together (*1 Cor 7:12–14*). Neither was he saying that Christians should shun the company of those who think differently from us. Were that to happen we would live in isolation and not be the salt and light in society that Jesus wants us to be (*Matt 5:13–16;1 Cor 5:9,10*). Although this Scripture has important truths for us to accept, Paul's concern was with the paganism in which the Corinthian church had to live.

Paul had good reason to believe that some converts had not broken with their pagan past completely and were still attending pagan temples, if only for social reasons (*cf. 1 Cor 10:14–23*). A number of them, he feared, had not broken free from some of the grosser pagan practices (*1 Cor 6:12–20*), and separation from that kind of company was essential. The apostle was right: righteousness and wickedness have nothing in common, fellowship is not possible between light and darkness and there is no harmony between Christ and Belial (*vv. 14b,15*). In company of that kind, we are there as witnesses for Christ, not to participate in their evil.

It was not possible for Paul to labour the negative aspects of discipleship without moving to more positive statements. He listed, therefore, a number of God's promises, commencing with, 'I will live with them and walk among them, and I will be their God, and they will be my people' (*v. 16b*). If we live in his presence and are aware of our special status in his eyes, surely, being separated from evil is no deprivation!

PRAYER

*I cannot evil actions do
When through this world I walk with you.
I cannot think in evil ways
When you have tuned my heart to praise.
When all I am is yours to use,
It is not hard your ways to choose.*

The Holy Spirit in Luke's Gospel
Luke 1:5–17

'Your wife Elizabeth will bear you a son, and you are to give him the name John . . . he will be filled with the Holy Spirit even from birth' (vv. 13b,15b, NIV).

As we approach Pentecost, with its dramatic record of the coming of the Holy Spirit to all who choose to receive him, we will look at some of the references to the work of the Spirit in Luke's Gospel. It is reasonable to assume that since Luke wrote the Acts of the Apostles, a book that could so easily be subtitled, 'The Acts of the Holy Spirit', his Gospel will provide us with additional insights into the work and nature of the third person in the Trinity. From the beginning of his Gospel, Luke gives a crucial place to the work of the Holy Spirit. Not that he is alone in this, of course, but we will follow Luke's references with profit.

Our key verses make reference to John the Baptist. When Zechariah was serving in the temple, he was visited by the angel of the Lord and told that his aged wife Elizabeth was to bear a son. Because of her age he could be forgiven for being a little sceptical. The son was to be a man of exceptional character and to be the forerunner of the Lord (v. 17), which explains why John was to be 'filled with the Holy Spirit' (v. 15). Without that aid he could not achieve the divine objective. The Holy Spirit has always enabled people to exceed their normal powers.

We note, also, that when the angel visited Mary and told her of her role in the birth of Christ, and she asked how this could be, she was told that the Holy Spirit 'will come upon you' (v. 35). Precisely what that meant we do not know, but we do know that the Holy Spirit is a creative Spirit. He was the agent of creation (Gen 1:2), and it was fitting that he should play a prime role in the coming of Christ, and in the new creation when men and women found new life in Jesus (5:17; John 16:7–15). When Mary visited Elizabeth, Luke records that she too 'was filled with the Holy Spirit' and was given special insights in consequence (vv. 41–45).

PRAYER *When heaven breaks through to human minds,*
The Holy Spirit bears the news.
His touch removes the veil that blinds,
Dispels the notions which confuse,
And lets us see what God has for us planned,
And gives the power to follow his command.

Jesus Presented in the Temple
Luke 2:21–40 (25–35)

'Now there was a man in Jerusalem called Simeon . . . He was waiting for the consolation of Israel, and the Holy Spirit was upon him' (v. 25, NIV).

It was required that every Jewish boy should be circumcised and named when he was eight days old and Mary and Joseph took Jesus to the Temple for these important ceremonies (*vv. 21–24*). The 'consolation of Israel' had reference to the dawn of the Messianic day, and Simeon had been promised that he would not die until he had seen the Messiah (*v. 26*). It is not surprising, therefore, that Simeon was waiting in the temple courts when Joseph and Mary arrived (*v. 27*). The aged and saintly Israelite took Jesus in his arms and blessed him (*vv. 28–32*).

The insights in Simeon's blessing indicated that he had been genuinely 'moved by the Spirit' (*v. 27a*). Although the Old Testament holds references to the worldwide intentions of God (*Gen 12:3; Isa 42:6–8; 49: 6*), Israel had become introverted and exclusive over many years, seeming to revel in its chosenness and disregard for other nations. The guidance of the Holy Spirit was very clear in Simeon's words. First, he recognised the Messiah; second, he knew that the Messiah was not only for Israel but for all the world; third, he had insights concerning the upheaval the Messiah would cause among his own people; and fourth, he knew the pain and sorrow that would come to Mary's heart (*vv. 29–35*).

The Holy Spirit is the great revealer and is especially the revealer of Jesus. When he, the Spirit, comes to us he speaks to our hearts about our needs and our Saviour. As with Simeon, and Anna who was present also on that occasion, the Spirit enables us to recognise Jesus. As Paul was to say much later, 'no-one can say, "Jesus is Lord," except by the Holy Spirit' (*1 Cor 12:3*). It is the Spirit also who teaches us that the gospel is for everyone. Simeon would know of the sinful excesses of the Gentile world of that day, but Christ had come for even the worst of people.

PRAYER   *You make your Spirit, Lord, available,*
              By him, you and the Saviour are made real.
              Through him, our hopes become attainable,
              And through his power you place on us your seal.
              All that you plan for us he can achieve,
              When once we fully trust you and believe.

John the Baptist

Luke 3:1–18

'John answered them all, "I baptise you with water. But one more powerful than I will come ... He will baptise you with the Holy Spirit and with fire" ' (v. 16, NIV).

As we have learned, John the Baptist was filled with the Holy Spirit from birth (*1:15*) and his unique lifestyle in the desert suggests his preparation by the Holy Spirit for a role of considerable importance. His arrival on the banks of the Jordan as a preacher of repentance and herald of the Messiah reveals the timing, relevance and public response we would expect from a man who was being directed by the Holy Spirit. John's bearing was that of a man who knew his place. He was single-minded, courageous, self-effacing, perceptive, articulate, convincing and effective: the ideal herald for the Messiah.

As the crowds gathered around him and were challenged by his message he made it clear that his baptism, although of great importance, was largely symbolic and was, therefore, incomplete. A more powerful than he would come who would baptise 'with the Holy Spirit and with fire'. The symbol would be replaced by the reality: the ceremonial rite give way to the creative energy of the life-giving Spirit. What a prospect!

Many attempts have been made to define the baptism of the Spirit and some very godly people define it differently. Some believe it happens at conversion; others hold that it is an experience which takes place at a later time. Others are persuaded that the baptism comes with the laying on of hands, a procedure which some people dispute; and there are those who are persuaded that the baptism is accompanied by the gift of tongues. These diverse opinions seem to indicate that the baptism of the Spirit is a very individual experience, and that the Holy Spirit comes to the open and responsive person in the way he, the Spirit, considers best. We can be sure that when he comes he will be careful to meet the specific needs of the heart and the requirements of the Lord Christ.

PRAYER　　　*O Holy Spirit, come with all your grace,*
　　　　　　　　And match the needs you find within my heart;
　　　　　　Make my rebellious heart a holy place,
　　　　　　　　And of Christ's body let me be a part.
　　　　　　With openness of heart and mind I bow,
　　　　　　And seek your promised baptism, just now.

Three Significant Words
Luke 3:1–18

'John answered them all, "I baptise you with water. But one more powerful than I will come, the thongs of whose sandals I am not worthy to untie. He will baptise you with the Holy Spirit and with fire" ' (v. 16, NIV).

There was a significance to those three words 'and with fire' which was beyond the knowledge of John the Baptist. Prophets often said things which meant more than they thought and this, surely, is a case in point. The baptism of the Holy Spirit was to mean the cleansing of the heart, the bestowal of spiritual gifts and a commissioning to fruitful service.

The context makes it clear that John had judgment in mind (*vv.* 7–14,17), but the experience of the Church has filled out these words immeasurably. Was John not, in true prophetic manner, referring to the way in which the Spirit enters the heart and turns hope for God into a real experience? Was he not also pointing to the zeal, the 'heart on fire' the disciple needs to pursue Christ's aims? And, surely, this Spirit-filled herald of Christ was indicating that ahead were fiery trials (*1 Pet 1:6–9*) which would test the faith until, like gold, it was purified by fire.

PRAYER

O gentle fire of God
Upon my soul descend,
Ignite the hopes which Godward turn,
Let faith to him ascend.

O searching flame of God,
With purifying fire
Cleanse me from sin's persistent stain;
Refine each vain desire.

O blazing flame of God,
Set my whole soul aflame
With love for Christ and steadfast zeal
His gospel to proclaim.

O altar flame of God,
Accept my offering
Of all I am and hope to be,
As all my life I bring.

The Baptism of Jesus (1)
Luke 3:21,22

'As he was praying, heaven was opened and the Holy Spirit descended on him in bodily form like a dove' (vv. 21b,22a, NIV).

The humility of Jesus is perfectly illustrated by the manner in which he submitted himself to the baptism of John. Crowds of Jews had pressed forward for John's baptism of repentance (*Matt 3:11*), a baptism which was out of character with Judaism insofar as Jews baptised only proselytes into their faith. Jesus, the sinless One, insisted on John baptising him also. The assumption is that Jesus presented himself for baptism in order to identify himself more closely with those whom he was destined to help, but God made of it a much more significant occasion.

We note that as Jesus was being baptised he was praying. No indication is given concerning the nature of his prayer, but it must have been related to his future. While he was praying we are told 'heaven was opened and the Holy Spirit descended on him', with consequences of enormous value to our needy world. Speculation concerning the coming of the Spirit to Jesus at his baptism has been substantial and we may never know its full importance; but it was an event of God's choosing, and God's strategies have never been inconsequential.

It is probably correct to say that whenever we pray heaven opens and the Holy Spirit comes to us in a special way. The eternal world, with its mystery, power and ability to satisfy the deepest needs of our hearts, always opens when we begin to pray. It was in Damascus, according to Luke's account (*Acts 9:10–19*) that, as Ananias was probably praying, the Lord came to him in a vision and told him about Saul the Church's persecutor, saying of him, 'for he is praying'. What marvellous things can happen when God's people are in prayer and when needy souls are in prayer also! On the occasion when heaven opened for Ananias and Saul, it proved to be one of history's greatest events.

PRAYER
If only I could understand
The wonder of your plans for me,
And know that heaven is near at hand,
With prayer a blessed heaven-opening key,
What glories would surround me day by day,
If I believed enough to really pray!

The Day of Pentecost

Acts 2:1–13

'When the day of Pentecost came, they were all together in one place. Suddenly a sound like the blowing of a violent wind came from heaven and filled the whole house where they were sitting' (v.1, NIV).

We must not press the idea too hard that heaven opens when we pray (*WoL 10 June 2000*) or we may be guilty of implying that heaven opens only when prayer is made, and that would be quite wrong. It opens much more often than we imagine. The tradition, however, that 120 believers who had gathered together were at prayer (*1:12–15*) is well-founded, and heaven most certainly opened for them. Indeed, it did so for all mankind on that special day. As with the Incarnation, circumstances had combined together perfectly and God sent his Spirit as he had promised. Heaven had opened yet again.

The Holy Spirit could have come silently as he has done so many times since, but we assume that on that historic occasion God acknowledged human weaknesses by making his coming dramatic and memorable. The sights and sounds impressed the senses of the disciples, and the gifts of power, courage and languages resulted in three thousand converts.

As we celebrate this great event today we do so in the knowledge that the Holy Spirit, who met the needs of the disciples on the Day of Pentecost, meets our needs today in the same wise and personal way. The sights and sounds of the Spirit's coming were unique to that occasion, but his power and relevance are not. We do not hear or see him coming but, by the changes he makes in our hearts and the gifts he lavishes upon us, we know that he is present with us, and that his power is at work within us. With awe, excitement and expectation we commemorate the Day of Pentecost and believe that God wants us to celebrate it every day.

PRAYER

If I remember, Lord, to ask at all,
I make petitions relatively small.
My prayers should match your generosity,
Reflect your trust in me, your will for me.
Dismiss my doubts, Lord, hear not what they say
And make today a Pentecostal day!

PRAYER SUBJECT   *For a great outpouring of God's Spirit today.*

The Baptism of Jesus (2)
Luke 3:21,22

'As he was praying, heaven was opened and the Holy Spirit descended on him in bodily form like a dove. And a voice came from heaven: "You are my Son, whom I love; with you I am well pleased" ' (vv. 21b, 22, NIV).

Our Lord's baptism was unique and, as we have already indicated, its major significance could well be lost on us (*WoL 10 June 2000*), but there are ways in which his baptism links with ours. Few of us have ever heard the Father's voice saying to us, 'You are my Son, whom I love; with you I am well pleased', but the wonderfully reassuring words the Father spoke to Jesus have been spoken to us by the Holy Spirit in his own way, and have been heard in the depths of our hearts.

When the Spirit comes to us he confirms our identity: we are indeed the children of God. When Paul wrote to the Galatians he said, 'Because you are sons, God sent the Spirit of his Son into our hearts, the Spirit who calls out, "*Abba*, Father" . . . and since you are a son, God has made you also an heir' (*Gal 4:6,7*). *The Spirit also confirms the Father's love for us.* Did not the apostle John say to the churches in Asia, 'How great is the love the Father has lavished on us, that we should be called children of God! And that is what we are!' (*1 John 3:1*)? And did not Jesus pray, 'May they [all believers] be brought to complete unity to let the world know that you sent me *and have loved them even as you have loved me*' (*John 17:23b*)? It is part of the Spirit's role to confirm that we are approved by God – that he is pleased with us. Paul begins one of his greatest passages of Scripture with the question that must always reassure us, 'If God is for us, who can be against us?' (*Rom 8:31*).

What the baptism of the Holy Spirit did for Jesus, to a lesser degree it does for us. The Holy Spirit is the third person in the Godhead, the one who makes God the Father and God the Son real to us (*John 16:14,15*). What wonderful ministries he exercises within our hearts!

PRAYER
Spirit of purity and grace,
Our weakness, pitying, see;
O make our hearts thy dwelling-place,
And worthier thee!

(Harriette Auber, SASB 200)

A Time of Testing
Luke 4:1–13

'Jesus, full of the Holy Spirit, returned from the Jordan and was led by the Spirit in the desert, where for forty days he was tempted by the devil' (vv. 1,2a, NIV).

It seems strange that immediately following his time of exaltation at the River Jordan, Jesus should be *led by the Spirit* into the desert there to be tested for some forty days. If, however, this time of stress does seem strange it is possible that our view on temptation needs amending. Some of us assume our difficulties arise because our spiritual life is low – when our hold on God is not as firm as it should be. But here we have Jesus 'full of the Holy Spirit', being 'led by the Spirit in the desert'. Perhaps we ought to add that we do sometimes face serious problems, many of them avoidable, when we have failed to nourish our spiritual life.

This, however, is one of the occasions when our English language is a little unhelpful to us. When we use the word 'tempt' it is almost always in the sense of enticement, a strong, sometimes irresistible encouragement to do wrong. But the Greek word which is translated 'tempt', as W.E. Vine points out, means 'to test, try, prove'. Since Jesus was being tempted by the devil it was obvious that *he* was seeking our Lord's downfall, but from the *Spirit's* angle, the temptations were there to test and prove Christ's newly confirmed status. Except we be tested how can we become strong? Except we learn to handle the problems and trials of life, how can we become mature?

Life tells us that often, when we have enjoyed a 'mountain-top experience,' we are plunged into the valley. If we are taking our Lord's experience of the Holy Spirit as a guide, we must note that when he was in the desert *he was no less full of the Spirit than before*. The rigours of the inhospitable desert, with its dramatic changes in temperature, lack of food and water, could have made Jesus feel isolated and bereft, but he knew who he was and trusted his Father accordingly.

PRAYER

When circumstances, Lord, are hard,
    And I am tempted, sorely stressed,
Help me to be upon my guard,
    And be made strong by each new test.
Give added strength for each adversity,
And faith to know your Spirit's life in me.

The Power of the Spirit
Luke 4:14–30

'Jesus returned to Galilee in the power of the Spirit ... He taught in their synagogues, and everyone praised him' (vv. 14a,15, NIV).

Tested, proved, and in the power of the Spirit, Jesus returned to Galilee and to the city where he had been raised from childhood (2:39). The people knew him as Joseph's son (*v. 22*), the carpenter's son (*cf. Matt 13:55*), and, knowing his family, they could not recognise him as the Messiah. If, as we have contended, the Holy Spirit confirms our identity (*WoL 12 June 2000*), sooner or later *the same Spirit confirms our destiny*. Jesus *was* a carpenter, but he was so much more than that – he was the fulfilment of the ancient prophecies and Saviour of the world. For what other reason would he say in his home town, in the synagogue where he had worshipped and been taught, 'The Spirit of the Lord is on me, because he has anointed me to preach good news to the poor ... to proclaim the year of the Lord's favour' (*vv. 18,19*)?

We are not misusing Scripture when we affirm that what the Spirit did for Jesus, to an amazing degree he does for us. Clearly, the Messiah role is his and not ours, but the Holy Spirit with whom our divine inheritance has been sealed (*Eph 1:13*) has made us part of the body of Christ (*1 Cor 12:27–30*) and Christ depends on us to fulfil our roles in his mission, namely the conversion and discipling of the world (*John 17:18*).

Employers may know us by our commercial qualifications; sons and daughters know us as parents; neighbours and friends know us as single, married or widowed. But though we remain whatever designation fits us, we are more than that. We have a God-given task to fulfil. We are ambassadors for Christ, channels of divine grace, and the source of much encouragement and truth to those around us. Ours is a glorious destiny. Although circumstances may limit our service, by the ministries of prayer and faith we are able to play our part in the Master's mission.

PRAYER

Come, O Spirit, come and guide me,
Show me my great destiny;
Walk my chosen way beside me,
Let my service fruitful be.
Naught matters but to do God's will,
His purpose for my life fulfil.

An Apprenticeship in Mission
Luke 10:1–24

'After this the Lord appointed seventy-two others and sent them two by two ahead of him to every town and place where he was about to go' (v. 1, NIV).

What a mission and what excitement! The group of twelve disciples was augmented by men who were part also of our Lord's travelling group and they were sent out on a mission. These additional missioners were close to him in spirit and it was Christ's long-term strategy that every follower would be engaged in his work. If it is felt that they had received little training for their task, it should be remembered that they had been in Jesus's company day after day, they had seen him at work and heard his teaching. They had been given his authority (*vv. 3–16*) and were, therefore, adequately equipped, as events were to prove (*v. 17*).

If, as we believe, the Holy Spirit confirms our identity (*WoL 12 June 2000*) and confirms our destiny (*WoL 14 June 2000*), it must be true to add that *he confirms our discipleship*. Those apprentice missioners went out knowing that, even though crowds gathered around their Master, they would be in a minority situation: 'the workers are few' (*v. 2b*). They knew also that many people would be hostile, hence the Lord's warning that they would be 'like lambs among wolves' (*v. 3*). Even so, Jesus had told them that the 'harvest is plentiful' (*v. 2a*). By that Jesus meant that a positive response awaited them. Inhospitable people there would be (*v. 10*) and some would receive them with hatred and intimidation (*v. 3*), but the victory would still be theirs (*vv. 8,9,16*).

With high hopes, a measure of fear, and as much faith as they could muster, the seventy-two went out. We can only assume that their experiences proved how right their Master was, and they returned with joy (*v. 17a*). Their discipleship had been validated by their success, a success they correctly ascribed to the Lord (*v. 17b*). The joy shared with Jesus was described as being 'through the Holy Spirit' (*v. 21*).

PRAISE
> *There is a special joy God gives*
> *To those who listen and obey;*
> *Who follow all Christ has to say*
> *Admitting no alternatives.*
> *When in his cause we every gift employ,*
> *His Holy Spirit gives abundant joy.*

Rejoicing in the Spirit
Luke 10:1–24 (17–24)

'Jesus, full of joy through the Holy Spirit' (v. 21a, NIV).

Because of our human limitations it is not possible for us to grasp the full meaning of the joy Jesus experienced on this and other occasions, but there must be merit in attempting to evaluate this special joy. Although our vocabulary cannot express that joy adequately, or our hearts experience it fully, we will grow spiritually as we try to understand. There must also be a connection between the joy experienced by the disciples as they returned from their mission (*v. 17*), and the joy of Jesus which, Luke tells us, was 'through the Holy Spirit' (*v. 21*).

There is a joy that is born of right relationships. Jesus was rightly related to God, his heavenly Father. All that he did was in obedience to him, and all that the Father had belonged to him because of this incredibly close relationship (*John 16:15*). Even in the Upper Room as he faced the horrors of crucifixion, our Lord's relationship with God was so secure that he was able to talk to the disciples about joy (*John 15:11; 16:20–24*). Through the ministry of Jesus we, too, are rightly related to the Father, and we also share the Father's joy (*cf. Matt 25:21b*).

There is a joy that is born of fruitful relationships. Jesus found so much satisfaction in his ministries to needy people. His disciples had been out on mission and great things had happened. Wisely they gave the glory to their Master (*v. 17*) but their joy was unlimited. And do we not know the sheer pleasure there is to be found in fruitful service?

There is a joy that is born of eternal relationships. The writer to the Hebrews wrote, 'for the joy set before him [Jesus] endured the cross' (*Heb 12:2*). He knew that his death on Calvary was not the end and, when *we* are born anew of the Spirit (*John 3:3–7*), we know that death is not the end. Indeed, our eternal life has already begun.

PRAYER
    On us let all thy grace be shown,
      Peace, righteousness and joy, and love –
    Thy kingdom – come to every heart,
    And all thou hast, and all thou art.

(*Charles Wesley*)

The Best of Gifts

Luke 11:1–13

'If you then, though you are evil, know how to give good gifts to your children, how much more will your Father in heaven give the Holy Spirit to those who ask him!' (v. 13, NIV).

Prayer has never been less than a privilege, often underused, much misunderstood, but a privilege of great value. Luke brings some of our Lord's teaching on prayer into this chapter and leaves us in no doubt that the God to whom we pray is our heavenly Father (*v. 2*). Even though Luke recounted the story of the man who tried to borrow bread from a friend at midnight, and received the loaves he wanted because of his importunity, we still do not receive a poor message concerning God. The parable is intended to teach the importance of boldness and persistence in prayer (*vv. 5–10*). Our prayers would be poorer if they lacked determination.

That unusual parable led to the questions Jesus posed to an hypothetical father (*v. 11*); questions so framed by our wise and loving Christ that they could be answered in one way only. These led on to our key verse, 'If you then, though you are evil, know how to give good gifts to your children, how much more will your Father in heaven give the Holy Spirit to those who will ask him!' (*v. 13*). God is our heavenly Father whose ways are wise, loving and righteous; it is unthinkable that he would not always be aware of our needs and constant in his desire to meet them. If earthly fathers treat their children well, God does much more.

Implicit in the text is the truth that the gift of the Holy Spirit is the supreme gift. When we have him, we have everything God has to offer us. Again we return to Christ's great words about the Spirit as recorded by John, 'He will bring glory to me by taking from what is mine and making it known to you. All that belongs to the Father is mine' (*John 16:14,15*). The Spirit, then, is the gift of gifts and, according to Jesus, the Father is more than willing to make the gift available to us (*v. 13b*).

PRAYER
Holy Spirit, power divine,
Fill and nerve this will of mine;
By thee may I strongly live,
Bravely bear, and nobly strive.

(Samuel Longfellow)

SUNDAY 18 JUNE

The Finger of God
Luke 11:14–20

'But if I drive out demons by the finger of God, then the kingdom of God has come to you' (v. 20, NIV).

Full of the Spirit, led by the Spirit and in the power of the Spirit (*4:1,14*), Jesus continued his ministry. By this time those who resented him, because they felt their status, livelihood or traditional religion were being threatened by his radical approach, sought every opportunity to discredit him. On this occasion Jesus had healed a dumb man. In those days it was commonly believed that a demon was responsible for afflictions of this nature, and Jesus drove out the demon (*v. 14*). Immediately, his detractors alleged that it was by the power of the prince of demons, Beelzebub, that the demon had been banished and the man cured (*v. 15*).

With much patience, Jesus answered their charge by pointing out that even Satan would not be so foolish as to declare war against one of his own subjects (*vv. 17,18*). He also asked a question concerning their own acts of healing: 'by whom do your followers drive them [demons] out?' (*v. 19*). Jesus continued with, 'But if I drive out demons by the finger of God, then the kingdom of God has come to you' (*v. 20*).

Our Lord's memorable metaphor, 'the finger of God', has interesting precedents. When Aaron produced the plague of gnats which Pharaoh's magicians could not replicate, the magicians said to Pharaoh, 'This is the finger of God' (*Exod 8:19*). It was the finger of God that wrote the ten commandments on the stone tablets (*Exod 31:18*), and created the heavens (*Ps 8:3*). The finger of God is the power of God. Indeed, Matthew believed the metaphor meant the Spirit of God (*Matt 12:28*). This evidence of divine power meant that the kingdom had actually come.

PRAYER

A miracle! Yes, a miracle!
God's Holy Spirit came
And we are not the same,
For he touched us
And filled us with his love.

(*Iva Lou Samples, SASB 215*)

PRAYER SUBJECT   *A greater awareness of the power of the Spirit.*

A Strong Warning
Luke 12:8–10

'Anyone who blasphemes against the Holy Spirit will not be forgiven'
(v. 10b, NIV).

This strong warning concerning blasphemy against the Holy Spirit is heightened because it follows our Lord's statement that anyone who sins against him can be forgiven (*v. 10a*). Each of the Gospels records some harsh, seemingly 'unforgivable' statements and acts against him but, said Jesus in effect, these are all forgivable. We wonder, therefore, where the line is drawn between sins against Jesus and sins against the Spirit. At some time or other, many Christians and would-be Christians have been anxious about this unforgivable sin.

Perhaps the solution to our anxiety is found in the charge made by our Lord's opponents that, 'By Beelzebub, the prince of demons, he [Jesus] is driving out demons' (*11:15*). Perhaps also there are some sins directed against Christ which, because of their wilfulness and blindness, become sins against the Holy Spirit, and this charge of casting out demons by the power of Beelzebub clarifies the issue for us.

It is possible for people to make so many evil choices in their life that the power of evil dominates them and renders them incapable of recognising goodness and truth. For such people – and, surely, the number is not great – their evil attitudes allow them to express an untruth with apparent conviction and sincerity. But we return to those who were witnesses to a miracle of healing by a Christ of compassion and compelling goodness. If ever anyone represented a righteous, loving God, Jesus did but, after observing his work and his goodness, those same people said that it was by 'Beelzebub, the prince of demons he is driving out demons' (*11:15*). Such blindness, with its inability to recognise light and goodness, is the sin against the Holy Spirit. It is the darkness of a lost soul who believes that darkness is light.

PRAYER
O Lord of mercy, truth and light,
Shine in my heart, dispel the night;
And let me always know and see
That Christ is all-in-all to me.
Keep my heart tender, Lord, my insight clear,
That faith and love might prove you always near.

Strong Encouragement
Luke 12:11,12

'For the Holy Spirit will teach you at that time what you should say' (v. 12, NIV).

It has been known for our key verse to be interpreted to mean that our Lord has guaranteed powerful speech at all times, thereby rendering preparation and hard work unnecessary. Such a viewpoint is clearly incorrect and overlooks the importance of the previous verse, 'When you are brought before synagogues, rulers and authorities, do not worry about how you will defend yourselves or what you will say' (v. 11). Our Lord's promise related to that kind of situation and not to any other.

The outworking of this promise was not long delayed. Shortly after the Day of Pentecost, Peter and John were brought before the synagogue rulers and authorities and asked, 'By what power or what name did you do this [healing the crippled beggar]?' (Acts 4:7b). Luke's account goes on, 'Then Peter, filled with the Holy Spirit, said to them' and there followed a powerful exposition of the Christian faith. Because Peter had no notice of the question he was asked, his impromptu reply was inspired by the Holy Spirit (Acts 4:1–22), exactly as Jesus had promised. Stephen's oration which preceded his martyrdom is another instance of the Holy Spirit giving aid when a believer was faced by the authorities (Acts 7:1ff.).

It must give great encouragement to a Christian under extreme difficulties to feel the eloquence of the Spirit welling up within. Confidence and courage must come also with the words. Furthermore, we cannot speak the thoughts of the Spirit without being aware that the Spirit, with all his other resources, is available. This awareness of the divine presence is, in all probability, a major factor in the experience of those who have endured persecution. Because Christians find themselves in testing situations it does not mean that they are inadequately filled with the Spirit or are ill-equipped to meet the demands; in fact, the opposite should be true. For him to teach us (v. 12), the Holy Spirit must be present.

PRAYER
I am so glad, Lord, for your wise provision
That will enable me to speak for you;
As I become involved in your great mission
I need to know that you will see me through.
And that with wisdom, power and eloquence,
I will proclaim the gospel's sure defence.

Continuity

Acts 1:1–8

'In my former book, Theophilus, I wrote about all that Jesus began to do and to teach' (v. 1, NIV).

The prologue to the Acts of the Apostles corresponds with the prologue to Luke's Gospel (*Luke 1:1–4*) and makes it clear that, from the outset, Luke anticipated a two-volume work. The first volume was related to the life and work of Jesus and the second volume to the beginnings and growth of the Church. We take note of the continuity Luke maintains between the power and glory of the resurrection (*Luke 24:45–53*) and the opening verses of the Acts of the Apostles: there is no loss of faith or optimism as we move from the first to the second volume. F.J. Foakes-Jackson commented, 'It may even be that the Third Gospel is not, so to speak, rounded off by the story of the Ascension, because to Luke the climax of the work of Jesus has never been reached. To him there can be no *finish* to the gospel in this world.' We would agree with that.

In common with the other Gospel writers Luke made significant contributions to our understanding of the person and work of the Holy Spirit, and his second volume reveals the Holy Spirit in action in a wide variety of ways. In Luke's mind, the gift of the Holy Spirit, promised from the earliest of days, promises which were reinforced by Jesus, was to be the supreme gift of the Father and Son to our world (*vv. 4,5*).

Concerning the interim period between his resurrection and ascension, Luke recorded that 'he [Jesus] was taken up to heaven, after giving instructions *through the Holy Spirit* to the apostles he had chosen' (*v. 2*). The italicised words indicate the mystery of the Godhead and the way chosen by the Father to reveal himself to mankind which was, and is, through the Son and the Spirit. Jesus, who was full of the Spirit, empowered by the Spirit, and who had received the Holy Spirit without limit (*Luke 4:1,14; John 3:34*) promised we would be baptised also (*v. 5*).

PRAYER

> *O Holy Spirit,*
> *Speaker of God's word to us,*
>   *Life of Christ within our hearts;*
> *Come with words victorious.*
>   *Bring the joy which love imparts,*
> *Make our poor hearts glorious.*

A Natural Resistance

Acts 1:1–8

'Do not leave Jerusalem, but wait for the gift my Father promised, which you have heard me speak about' (v. 4b, NIV).

What amazing days followed the resurrection of our Lord! To the euphoria of the resurrection of Jesus was added his frequent appearances to his disciples and the teaching he gave. They were in preparation for one of history's greatest undertakings, and the task Jesus had in mind for them must have heightened their perceptions and expectations. Even so, they displayed resistance to change insofar as they held stubbornly to their old ideas of the kind of kingdom Jesus was to inaugurate. As Jesus was looking ahead to the establishment of the kingdom of God on earth, they were still looking for the restoration of Israel's former glory.

The disciples should have been agog with the command Jesus gave them: 'wait for the gift my Father promised' (*v. 4*) but, as Luke recorded, when they came together again they asked, 'Lord, are you at this time going to restore the kingdom to Israel?' (*v. 6*). If ever a group of men needed the baptism of the Holy Spirit, it was that group.

We have referred to the baptism of the Spirit in connection with our Lord's baptism by John (*WoL 12 June 2000*) but the presence of the promise in our chosen passage requires that we add a little more. Dr. I. Howard Marshall, with direct reference to the outpouring of the Spirit in baptism, wrote, 'No one synonym [i.e. outpouring] can do justice to its range of meaning as a Christian technical term for the reception of the Spirit.' There are certain things the Holy Spirit does for us all when he comes to us, some of which have been mentioned previously, but there are some personal things he does for us which he does not need to do for other people. This could be related to our personalities or to the task he wants us to do. Sufficient it is for us to say that there is no limit to his power to change and equip us. What a glorious provision this is!

PRAYER

> *Breathe on me, Breath of God,*
> *Till I am wholly thine,*
> *Until this earthly part of me*
> *Glows with thy fire divine.*

(Edwin Hatch, SASB 189)

A Renewed Promise
Acts 1:6–9

'But you will receive power when the Holy Spirit comes on you; and you will be my witnesses in Jerusalem, and in all Judea and Samaria, and to the ends of the earth' (v. 8, NIV).

Jesus was not to be drawn by the disciples when they asked him about restoring the kingdom to Israel – that was in the Father's hands (*v. 7*) – but he had a very positive, life-changing, world-changing word for them, as our key verse indicates. They would receive power after the Holy Spirit had come to them. In previous studies we have noted the ordinariness of the disciples and concluded that this common characteristic is part of the divine strategy. God has always intended to work through ordinary people knowing that his Spirit would make them extraordinary. The promise of power was made, therefore, because it was essential.

We note the obvious, that the Spirit with which Jesus was baptised is the Spirit with which they and, subsequently, all believers were to be baptised. The power Jesus had to such a degree is the power we have to a lesser degree. The Greek word which stands behind our word 'power' includes, according to Strong's definition, a 'miraculous element'. The definition includes also 'abilities, abundance, meaning, strength and mighty works'. As we have noted elsewhere, the Spirit's gift is unlimited. The Spirit imparts initiative, boldness, authority and powers of persuasion. We have only to compare the failure of the apostle Peter, in the courtyard when he was challenged about his relationship with Jesus (*Luke 22:54–62*), with his bold proclamation of the Resurrection outside the Upper Room on the day of Pentecost, to see the change the Spirit makes. How greatly we need the power, the fire of the Holy Spirit today!

PRAYER

> 'Tis fire we want, for fire we plead,
>   Send the fire!
> The fire will meet our every need,
>   Send the fire!
> For strength to ever do the right,
> For grace to conquer in the fight,
> For power to walk the world in white,
>   Send the fire!

(*William Booth, SASB 203*)

The Everlasting Command
Acts 1:1–11

'You will receive power when the Holy Spirit comes on you; and you will be my witnesses in Jerusalem, and in all Judea and Samaria, and to the ends of the earth' (v. 8, NIV).

When Jesus made this command he ascended into heaven and two angels appeared who told the disciples that Jesus would return 'in the same way you have seen him go into heaven' (v. 11). The disciples would know that our Lord's return to heaven and future return to earth were crucial elements in the Father's strategy.

Another crucial part of God's plan was that believers were to fulfil the role of witnesses. There would be exceptionally gifted people who would do remarkable things (cf. 1 Cor 12:1ff.) but witnessing for Jesus would be the role for every disciple. The strategy was relatively simple: the Holy Spirit would baptise and by that baptism would impart power, and from newly empowered lives would flow the witness that would change the hearts of family members, neighbours and friends. Since the disciples were in Jerusalem, it followed that they would be Christ's witnesses in that great city and the witness would spread elsewhere.

The church in Jerusalem could not have foreseen how the spread would occur. After the Church was established Stephen was captured and brought to face the Sanhedrin (6:8–12). His eloquent witness resulted in his martyrdom (7:1ff.) and on that same day persecution, of which Saul of Tarsus was a part, broke out against the Church. Church members fled to other parts of Judea and Samaria and continued to witness (8:1–8). Later, soon after the conversion of Saul, the Holy Spirit led the church in Antioch to commission Saul and Barnabas to take the gospel to other lands (13:1–5). In due time, Saul – now Paul – was led by the Spirit to take his group, which included Luke, and preach the gospel in Europe (16:6–10). Christianity was becoming a world religion.

PRAYER   *Give me thy strength, O God of power,*
Then winds may blow, or thunders roar,
Thy faithful witness will I be;
'Tis fixed, I can do all through thee.

(*Johann Joseph Winckler, trs John Wesley, SASB 526*)

The All-pervading Spirit

Acts 1:12–26

'They all joined together constantly in prayer, along with the women and Mary the mother of Jesus, and with his brothers' (v. 14, NIV).

After our Lord's ascension and the encounter with the angels, the disciples returned to the Upper Room in Jerusalem there to meet a substantial group of other believers. In addition to the eleven apostles, there were the women, Mary the Lord's mother, and his brothers. The total number present was about 120 (*v. 15*). We note that they were 'constantly in prayer'. Luke's account gives the impression that they concentrated on prayer. There must, however, have been excitement and wonder in the air at the presence of some who counted themselves as believers, not least the brothers of our Lord, whose names are elsewhere given as James, Joseph, Judas and Simon (*Mark 6:3*).

Although the promise of the Spirit's coming awaited fulfilment, the Holy Spirit *was* there, directing and inspiring them. They could not pray – as we cannot pray – except moved by the Holy Spirit. We cannot even call Jesus Lord unless the Holy Spirit moves us (*1 Cor 12:3b*). He is our motivator and, when we are unable to express our needs, he speaks for us (*Rom 8:26*). In the believers' desire to pray and the fellowship they shared in prayer, the Holy Spirit was the prime mover.

We note also that Peter referred to the Holy Spirit speaking through the mouth of David using words which, in Peter's judgment, fitted the situation created by Judas (*Pss 69:25; 109:8*). On the basis of that inspiration the disciples elected Judas's replacement. Not only is the Holy Spirit our inspiration in the art of prayer, he is also the means whereby Scripture becomes relevant to us and powerful in our lives. He is the all-pervading Spirit who is our constant guide and teacher (*John 16:13*).

PRAYER

> *O send thy Spirit, Lord,*
> *Now unto me,*
> *That he may touch my eyes*
> *And make me see.*

(Alexander Groves, SASB 650)

PRAYER SUBJECT   *A greater dependence on the Holy Spirit in prayer.*

Outward and Inward Signs
Acts 2:1–21

'All of them were filled with the Holy Spirit and began to speak in other tongues as the Spirit enabled them' (v. 4, NIV).

Luke's account of the baptism of our Lord is given in a low-key style; he described the event simply without recourse to cheap dramatic effects or language (*Luke 3:21–23*). By so doing he makes it believable to us. His account of the coming of the Spirit to the disciples and the world is handled with similar restraint. The dramatic elements relate to the facts, not to the language describing them. We have no sense of being manipulated into accepting an event which could owe more to imagination and presentation than to reality. The outward signs both for Christ's baptism and that of the disciples on the Day of Pentecost are credible. The ability of the disciples to speak in other tongues so that people from other parts of the world knew what they were saying was important (*v. 6*). The gospel is for all people and all nations. The coming of the Spirit, so long prophesied, and so full of potential for all mankind, could hardly happen without some special characteristic to mark its significance.

The inward signs related to the Spirit's coming on the Day of Pentecost are visible and credible also. Perhaps foremost and most obviously was the courage it gave the disciples. Not very long before they had been in hiding because of their allegiance to Jesus (*John 20:19*) but now without delay they left the Upper Room, spilled out on to the street, and Peter gave a speech of authority and power. His hearers were left in no doubt concerning their complicity in Christ's death (*v. 23*). The Spirit gives courage to witness, as we can confirm when we ourselves have been made courageous in our witness for the Master. As a natural leader, Peter must have been a good natural communicator but, as we study his address, we note the rare quality of his speech. The Holy Spirit had gifted him and released him. His first sermon was a masterpiece of construction and convicting power.

PRAYER   *There is a clarity of mind*
          Which comes when hearts are confident;
      When grace has proved not hard to find,
          And self becomes subservient.
      The Spirit stands behind that clarity,
      Imparting truth with power and charity.

TUESDAY 27 JUNE

Authority

Acts 2:22–37

'Men of Israel, listen to this' (v. 22a, NIV).

As we try to imagine that world-changing event which took place on the Day of Pentecost, we visualise Peter standing in front of the immense crowd which, almost as miraculously as the event itself, had gathered quickly. It is the way Peter stamped his authority on the scene that catches the eye. He commenced his address with the diplomatic, 'Fellow Jews and all you who live in Jerusalem, let me explain this to you; listen carefully to what I say' (*v. 14*). But almost in the next breath we hear him saying, 'Men of Israel, listen to this' (*v. 22a*). Peter's authority was now established and that authority was from the Holy Spirit.

All that Jesus had told them in the Upper Room seven short weeks earlier was true. As Jesus, full of the Spirit and in the Spirit's power, had been sent into the world, so had Peter and the others (*John 17:18*). Jesus gave the commission, the Spirit gave them the power. It was an irresistible combination then and remains an irresistible combination to this day.

Our roles within the mission of Christ may not be to stand in front of a great company and demand a hearing with our equivalent of 'Men of Israel, listen to this', but the Spirit's baptism has given us authority enough for our situation. We noted earlier (*WoL 24 June 2000*) that God's strategy is that believers should witness. We are to share with someone else what Christ has done for us. The power has been imparted and, however diffident we may feel, the moment we commence to witness our confidence will grow. The Holy Spirit will see to that. Furthermore, in many instances, our authority will be recognised. Experience teaches us that when we stay within the realm of personal witness we are given a hearing. It is when we try to be what we are not, and speak with authority on something we do not know and have not proved, that our difficulties begin. We have all the authority we need to do our task.

PRAYER

Help me, O Lord, my faith to share,
*   To tell what you have done for me.*
Give me the courage, Lord, to dare,
*   To witness how you set me free.*
However faltering be my word,
I know you want it to be heard.

Fruitfulness (1)

Acts 2: 22–41

'When the people heard this, they were cut to the heart and said to Peter and the other apostles, "Brothers, what shall we do?" ' (v. 37, NIV).

Few sermons in world history can have been as fruitful as Peter's first challenge to his own people. Such was the power of it that men, some of whom must have been strongly opposed to Jesus, were 'cut to the heart'. By the end of the day three thousand people had been added to the Church. We assume that at the beginning of the day the Church numbered approximately 120 people and, within 12 hours, had increased by 2,500 per cent. That was fruitfulness indeed!

Fruitfulness is rather more complex, however, than a superficial counting of heads suggests. In a most remarkable way, the gift of the Spirit had made Peter Christ's man in a way he had not been previously. In the courtyard where he had failed so badly (*Luke 22:54–62*), the imagined consequences of confessing Christ counted for much with him thereby causing his failure but, after the Spirit had come upon him, he manifested a deep unconcern for himself. If there were to be serious consequences to this Day of Pentecost witness, Peter would witness and leave the rest with God. Whatever had been lacking in Peter's spiritual life earlier had been supplied by the Holy Spirit. Of difficult circumstances he was to write later, 'rejoice that you participate in the sufferings of Christ, so that you may be overjoyed when his glory is revealed' (*1 Pet 4:13*).

We note the way in which our Lord's promises concerning the gift of the Spirit were fulfilled. Jesus had said, 'the Counsellor, the Holy Spirit, whom the Father will send in my name, will teach you all things and will remind you of everything I have said to you' (*John 14:26*). Peter's passionate presentation bears the hallmark of a mind greater than his own. The quotation from Joel (*vv. 17–21*) he might have known, but the quotes from the Psalms (*vv. 25–28*) suggest the work of the Spirit within him.

PRAYER   *So often, Lord, I trust my own resources,*
            And work as though I laboured all alone,
        Forgetful that your Spirit reinforces
            All I should do: all you desire to own.
        Remind me, Lord, that in my work for you,
        Your Holy Spirit's power will see me through.

Fruitfulness (2)

Acts 2:22–41

'When the people heard this, they were cut to the heart and said to Peter and the other apostles, "Brothers, what shall we do?" ' (v. 37, NIV).

One of the reasons why Peter was so sure that Jesus was exalted was because the Holy Spirit, whom Jesus had received (*Luke 3:21,22*), had now been poured out on them, 'he [Jesus] has received from the Father the promised Holy Spirit and *has poured out what you now see and hear*' (*v. 33*). In fact, so confident was Peter concerning the exaltation of Jesus that he said, 'God has made this Jesus . . . both Lord and Christ' (*v. 36*). This was Holy Spirit inspiration – not a human deduction.

Developing further the supernatural element in this matter of communication, we note one of the remarkable ways in which the Holy Spirit works. He was in Peter, guiding his thoughts, lifting his perceptions to hitherto undreamed-of heights and giving him the ability to declare the mysteries of God with authority and clarity. But, wonderfully, the Holy Spirit was in Peter's hearers also. The message the apostle delivered went straight to the heart and produced deep conviction. We can only marvel at the way in which the Holy Spirit inspires the message and the messenger and, at the same time, stimulates, disturbs, and quickens the hopes of the hearer. In this latter regard, Jesus said this would happen: 'When he [the Holy Spirit] comes, he will convict the world of guilt in regard to sin and righteousness and judgment' (*John 16:8*). That is precisely the ministry the Spirit exercised then and has continued to exercise.

When God's people make their witness something always happens in the hearts of their hearers. Sometimes, not as often as we desire, the words go straight to the heart and conversion follows. Sometimes the witness made will be one of many before that desired result occurs. For hardened listeners our witness enables people to hear the gospel in order to accept or reject it. Sadly, so many reject our Lord (*John 3:18*).

PRAYER   *Lord, speak through me;*
Grant to my words authority.
And plant within that listening soul
A longing to be fully whole.
Yours is the power, O Lord, the love, the will,
Now use me, your great purpose to fulfil.

A Verifiable Argument
Acts 2:22–24, 36–39

'Repent and be baptised, every one of you, in the name of Jesus Christ for the forgiveness of your sins. And you will receive the gift of the Holy Spirit' (v. 38, NIV).

J.A. Findlay made the observation that no one attempted to argue against Peter during his Day of Pentecost speech. It is true that some 'made fun of them' saying, 'they have had too much wine' (*v. 13*) but not a voice was raised to challenge the statements Peter made concerning the death and resurrection of Jesus or to deny the guilt of those who had crucified him. This is remarkable because it was in the material interests of many people to prove that Jesus was a failure.

Perhaps the great crowd, which had gathered because of the mysterious sounds associated with the coming of the Spirit (*vv. 2,6*), was aware of the closeness of the spiritual world and felt that they may have been witnesses to a divine visitation. That is mere speculation but of this we can be sure: there was an atmosphere around the event which stilled contentious spirits and made it easier for truth to be accepted. Not everything, but much of what Peter said, was verifiable. The arguments against the resurrection of Jesus had been in circulation for seven weeks (*Matt 27:62–66*). If the resurrection was a story fabricated by the disciples there were enough people in Jerusalem to disprove it. The truth seems to be clear: Jesus was risen and, that being so, further dramatic events could be expected such as the fulfilment of Joel's prophecy (*vv. 16–21*).

The verification was before the eyes of the crowd that the disciples, who had not been courageous at the crucifixion, were now witnessing with boldness. Furthermore, when the people asked 'what shall we do?' (*v. 37b*) and Peter told them to 'Repent and be baptised in the name of Jesus', he made also the promise that the Holy Spirit would come upon them (*v. 38*). This was a promise capable of immediate verification. They could prove it to be true, or untrue, that very day.

PRAYER   *Your promises, Lord, can be verified;*
We are not left uncertainly to wait
For distant circumstance to consummate
The promises you made before you died.
Your Resurrection made each promise sure,
And through your Spirit we are now secure.

The Completeness of the Gift

Acts 2:36–41

'And you will receive the gift of the Holy Spirit' (v. 38, NIV).

Some scholars, for a number of reasons, are a little puzzled by the inclusion of baptism in Peter's formula for salvation: one being that very shortly afterwards when he called upon the people to repent it is omitted (*cf. 3:11–26*). Another reason is that John, to whose water baptism Peter may have been referring, said, 'I baptise you with water. But one more powerful than I will come . . . He will baptise you with the Holy Spirit' (*Luke 3:16*). Again, there are those who believe that the statement simply means that people are to repent of their sins, believe in Jesus for forgiveness and they will be baptised by the Holy Spirit. Peter may have had in mind total immersion or a more symbolic baptism, but the fact is clear that without faith in Jesus, there can be no baptism of the Spirit.

We take note of the firmness and extent of the promise. The gift of the Spirit is for 'all whom the Lord our God will call' (*v. 37*). At that precise moment Peter was addressing 'God-fearing Jews' (*vv. 5,6*) who may well have thought only of the Jews who lived in distant lands, but the promise was so much greater than that. Experience was to prove that the promise far exceeded their ability to imagine at that stage. For Peter to say that they would receive the very Spirit he and the other disciples had received was true, but the Spirit comes to each man and woman in a very personal way which makes his coming quite distinctive.

Some people have very deep wounds, having suffered much physically or psychologically. Many have been physically abused, humiliated and made to feel worthless; others have sinned in ways which have left deep flaws in the character. Although we look very much like each other, inwardly we are quite different; but when the Spirit comes he heals our wounds and makes us whole. He is the Counsellor, who speaks peace and wisdom to our hearts. He is God's answer to our frailty.

PRAISE
> *My heart, O Lord, has always known*
> *That somehow you would meet my needs,*
> *Empower me for godly deeds,*
> *Make sure my gods are overthrown.*
> *Your Spirit's baptism of love and fire,*
> *Is everything my flawed heart could desire.*

An Unusual Parable
Luke 16:1–14

'I tell you, use worldly wealth to gain friends for yourselves, so that when it is gone, you will be welcomed into eternal dwellings' (v. 9, NIV).

This is not the easiest parable to understand because it seems to be commending dishonesty (*v. 8*), but it may be easier to understand if we read it with a heightened awareness of its context. Jesus had been speaking to a crowd which included Pharisees and teachers of the law who had been saying to each other, 'This man welcomes sinners, and eats with them' (*15:2*). It was in response to that criticism that Jesus told the parables of the lost sheep, the lost coin and the lost son (*15:3ff.*). Although the next chapter opens with, 'Jesus told his disciples' (*16:1; cf. NASB*), it is clear that the crowd was still there and those who were near to him heard what he said. This included the Pharisees who, in our Lord's eyes, were people who loved money for its own sake (*vv. 13,14*).

Among the religious leaders of that day, the Pharisees were not alone in this approach to wealth. Our Lord cleared the temple of those who had turned the Father's house 'into a market' (*John 2:16*) and that unseemly business was owned and run by the chief priests and their families.

Jesus well knew the snares that come with wealth. He spoke of the 'deceitfulness of wealth' (*Mark 4:19b*) and, when the rich young ruler turned away from him our Lord said, 'How hard it is for the rich to enter the kingdom of God!' (*18:24*). Even so, although Jesus possessed no material wealth (*cf. 9:58*), he was concerned not so much about wealth itself as about what wealth can do to people. The Pharisees were a case in point; they loved wealth for its own sake. Paul, following his Master and himself owning nothing, wrote to Timothy, 'For the love of money is a root of all kinds of evil' (*1 Tim 6:10*). Times have changed little.

PRAYER

O let me love you, Lord, with all my heart,
With all my strength, my mind and all my soul;
And let me with all covetousness part,
Surrendering to you my life's control.
I do not need a heart which longs for wealth,
But need a heart which finds in you its health.

PRAYER SUBJECT   *Victims of ethnic cleansing.*

A Lost Advantage
1 Kings 11:1–13

'His heart was not fully devoted to the LORD his God, as the heart of David his father had been' (v. 4b, NIV).

We return to the story of King Solomon (*WoL 4 Mar 2000*) whose kingship was given such a marvellous start. He was a many-talented man and, having been granted wisdom by God, had the pleasure of seeing the kingdom he had inherited from his distinguished father grow in every way. Solomon had even been granted two visions of God (*3:5; 9:2,3*). Other nations respected him and the remarkable Queen of Sheba visited him. Her generous tribute to Solomon included the words, 'Because of the Lord's eternal love for Israel, he has made you king, to maintain justice and righteousness' (*10:9b*). Alas! Power corrupts; praise and adulation warp the judgment (*10:23,24*); political expediency weakens principles (*3:1*); tolerance of idol worship erodes loyalty to the worship of the true God (*v. 4a*); and Solomon began to sin. In the historian's judgment, 'Solomon did evil in the eyes of the Lord' (*v. 6a*).

When Solomon broke the law of God by marrying into forbidden nations (*v. 1*), he opened the door to even greater sins. How could he deny his wives the right to their own forms of worship? How could he refuse to allow shrines to their gods to be erected? Having allowed these two concessions it was not a large step to engaging in idol worship himself (*vv. 4–8*). To tolerate the presence of idols on Israel's soil was sinful enough, but to connive at idol worship was even worse.

For a man who had been given so much and whose life was so full of promise, the final years of Solomon were an enormous tragedy. He could have occupied a place in Jewish history comparable in honour to that of his father, instead of which his wisdom turned to folly and, by his conduct, the kingdom was destined for decline. 'From everyone who has been given much,' said Jesus, 'much will be demanded' (*Luke 12:48*).

PRAYER
Help me to live in true simplicity,
In complete trust and full obedience;
Save me from weakness and complicity
In wrongful worship and impenitence.
I would in faith pursue my pilgrim way,
And grow in love and wisdom every day.

A Great Potential

1 Kings 11:14–41 (26–40)

'Now Jeroboam was man of standing, and when Solomon saw how well the young man did his work, he put him in charge of the whole labour force of the house of Joseph' (v. 28, NIV).

Even during Solomon's reign there had been opposition to him for which he was not responsible. The seeds of hatred sown by Joab's massacre in Edom and David's destruction of his enemies in Zobah bloomed unpleasantly in the country (*vv. 14–25*). In Jeroboam, however, Solomon was about to reap the harvest of his own folly. Jeroboam was a man of great ability who had earned the respect of his peers, and Solomon recognised this ability by giving Jeroboam an important role in a large building project. In the king's eyes, Jeroboam was a man for the future.

Solomon was not the only one who had recognised the great potential of Jeroboam: in God's eyes also, Jeroboam was a man to cultivate. As part of God's plan, Jeroboam was waylaid by the prophet Ahijah. The prophet was wearing a new cloak and, to dramatise the message he had for Jeroboam, Ahijah removed his new garment and tore it into twelve pieces, each piece being representative of a tribe of Israel. Ahijah then revealed that God intended Jeroboam to reign over ten tribes (*v. 31*) and Solomon's son would reign over one tribe (*v. 32*). The arithmetical error is slightly confusing because we know that the southern kingdom was to consist of the tribes of Judah and Benjamin (*cf. 12:21*).

The plan God had for Jeroboam was breathtaking: he was to be the king of Israel with a dynasty akin to that of David. Understandably, God's promise was conditional upon Jeroboam being obedient to his statutes and commands (*v. 38*). This was a condition that ought not to have posed too many problems for Jeroboam, insofar as his potential would be fully developed in the process. It is understandable, also, that when Solomon learned of all this, Jeroboam fled to Egypt (*v. 40*).

PRAYER   *You know my limitations, Lord,*
                The many things I cannot do:
            But you know my potential, Lord,
                The dreams to be fulfilled through you.
            Enlarge my view, increase my faith and power,
            That I might serve you better from this hour.

How to Lose a Kingdom (1)

1 Kings 12:1–24 (1–17)

'So they sent for Jeroboam, and he and the whole assembly of Israel went to Rehoboam and said to him: "Your father put a heavy yoke on us, but now lighten the harsh labour and the heavy yoke he put on us, and we will serve you" ' (vv. 3,4, NIV).

Rehoboam was the son and heir of Solomon, and Jeroboam was the man whose great potential had been recognised by both God and the king. Jeroboam had escaped to Egypt (*11:40*) returning only on the death of Solomon (*v. 2*). Even though Jeroboam had been told by the prophet that he would be king (*11:37*), he still went with the people to Rehoboam to offer allegiance under certain reasonable conditions (*vv. 3,4*).

Wisely, Rehoboam sought the advice of his elders who knew how Solomon had oppressed his people. In their considered opinion, the sensible course to follow was to accept the offer made (*vv. 6,7*). Foolishly, Rehoboam rejected their counsel and turned to his peers who, seemingly, were as spoilt and immature as himself. Their advice was to intensify the pressure on the people (*vv. 8–11*). What made them think, we wonder, that a people labouring under a strong sense of grievance would submit to more oppression? Stupidly, Rehoboam did as the young men advised and told the reassembled tribes that he would be a greater taskmaster than his father had ever been (*vv. 12–15*). Having alienated the ten tribes who had been promised to Jeroboam, Rehoboam returned to his two tribes, having lost the major part of his kingdom (*vv. 16,17*).

Rehoboam made two attempts to reassert his authority over the ten tribes. Adoniram, a successor to Jeroboam as the man in charge of forced labour, lost his life in the process, and Rehoboam narrowly escaped death (*v. 18*). Undeterred, Rehoboam gathered an army together to attack Israel but God spoke through Shemaiah, a prophet, ordering them to disband (*vv. 22–24*). The kingdom that had been united under David and Solomon was now divided for all time.

PRAYER
> Why do we think, O Lord,
>   That we are much more wise than you?
>   That human minds and hands can do
> Much better though our minds are flawed?
>   Persuade us, Lord, that in the end,
>   We must upon your power depend.

How to Lose a Kingdom (2)
1 Kings 12:25–33

'After seeking advice, the king made two golden calves. He said to the people, "It is too much for you to go up to Jerusalem. Here are your gods, O Israel, who brought you up out of Egypt" ' (v. 28, NIV).

What utter folly! Jeroboam had been promised the ten tribes who were to make up the northern kingdom of Israel on condition that he did all that God commanded him (*11:38*), and almost the first thing he did was to make idols for his people to worship. The new king's problem was quite obvious. If Jerusalem was the religious centre to which his people had to go for the festivals Rehoboam, his rival, could continue to influence them and Jeroboam would be disadvantaged thereby (*vv. 26,27*). Jeroboam's simple solution was to create worship centres in the new kingdom in order to establish independence for the ten tribes, but God would have given the king a better solution than the one he found. Jeroboam could have reasoned that if God was powerful enough to give him the kingdom in the first place, he was powerful enough to keep his kingdom intact, regardless of any advantages Jerusalem might have.

It seemed to be foolish, also, to make two golden calves for the people to worship (*vv. 28–30*). Had Jeroboam forgotten his history and the golden calves Aaron had made at Sinai? (*Exod 32:1ff.*) Scholars, however, tell us that Jeroboam might not have been quite as foolish as we imagine because it was common among other nations for golden bulls to be made, and for the people to believe that their invisible gods were standing on the backs of the animals. But Israel worshipped a living God and Jeroboam, God's appointed king, should have known better.

Jeroboam had been promised a kingdom comparable with that of the great King David if, like David, he kept God's commands (*11:37,38*). But he had by his disobedience guaranteed that he would lose everything. Once again, the love of power had changed a man's priorities.

PRAYER
True power is not found in the exercise
  Of self-love and self-oriented ways.
The people who are powerful and wise
  Are those who give to God their love and praise.
We have a Father-God whose word is sure,
And in whose purposes we are secure.

Kings and Prophets
1 Kings 13:1–10

'By the word of the LORD a man of God came from Judah to Bethel, as Jeroboam was standing by the altar to make an offering. He cried out against the altar by the word of the LORD: "O altar, altar! This is what the Lord says" ' (vv. 1,2a, NIV).

From this point onwards the books of Kings are dominated by the names of the kings of Israel and Judah and the swift repetition of unfamiliar names tends to confuse us. About this confusion we need not be unduly perturbed; of greater concern is the fact that, in the main, the rulers of God's people were evil men who caused the people to sin. God's judgment lies heavily on the records of these kings who, given the opportunity to write themselves in history as God's representatives, chose instead to oppose God and live evil, shameful lives. Jeroboam, he who had been promised and given so much, was as great an offender as any other. Ahijah the prophet, who had told Jeroboam of his great prospects (11:29–39), must have been bewildered by the new king's failures.

We note, however, that God did not leave himself without witnesses. Although the Scriptures reveal the wickedness of Israel's rulers, they show also the dedication and courage of the men of God. Ahijah shared with Jeroboam God's vision for him (11:29), Shemaiah defied the immature Rehoboam (12:22–24) and, as our key passage shows, an unnamed man of God challenged Jeroboam as he stood at the altar (vv. 1,2). What courage this anonymous prophet displayed!

With a fine, dramatic touch the man of God addressed the altar rather than king or people. From Israel's earliest days God's men had built altars (Gen 12:8; 28:18) and, under Moses, the altar became central to their worship. The prophet could not have chosen a more powerful way of making God's priorities clear to the nation, priorities made even more certain by the signs which were soon to follow.

TO PONDER

The altar of the Lord should be kept pure;
Unworthy offerings never should be made.
The altar flame of God burns bright and sure
And those misusing it should be afraid,
Because both flame and altar are the Lord's,
And ultimately, no one God defrauds.

Impressed but Not Convinced
1 Kings 13:1–10

'That same day the man of God gave a sign: "This is the sign the Lord has declared: The altar will be split apart and the ashes on it will be poured out" ' (v. 3, NIV).

If the assembled people anticipated drama they were not to be disappointed. The anonymous man of God (*but see 2 Chron 13:22*) proceeded to prophesy to the effect that a son by the name of Josiah would be born who would burn the bones of Israel's pagan priests on that very altar (*v. 2b*), a prophecy soon to be fulfilled (*2 Kgs 23:15–16; cf. Lev 26:30*). The prophet confirmed his authority by giving the sign that the altar would split and its ashes be poured out on the ground. With mounting anger, Jeroboam pointed to the man of God, ordering that he be seized, whereupon the outstretched arm became fixed and shrivelled (*v. 4b*), an evidence of God's disdain for the puny power of the king.

More was to follow: the prophecy concerning the destruction of the altar was fulfilled immediately. Aware of the divine power and his own helplessness, Jeroboam asked the man of God to intercede for him with '*your* God' in order that his limb would be restored (*v. 6*). Even the restored shrivelled limb failed to convince the king of his wrongdoing.

With his understanding of the human heart and knowledge of Hebrew history, our Lord was sceptical about the power of signs to move people towards faith in God (*Matt 16:1–4*). Jeroboam should have been convinced by the accuracy of the prophecy and the withering and healing of his hand that God was real and could not be ignored. But the best Jeroboam seemed able to do was to invite the man of God back to the palace for a meal and to receive a gift (*v. 7*). He should have asked the prophet how God planned to establish Israel's independence from Judah and the Jerusalem temple. No doubt God had such a strategy in mind, but Jeroboam's heart was not set on God. Even the powerful signs shown by the prophet failed to convince him that he must change.

PRAYER   *How arrogant becomes the pagan mind!*
                 With pointed finger men would God command.
            But, late or soon, eventually find
                 That their affairs are subject to God's hand.
            Though we feel free Almighty God to oppose,
            The truest freedom in obedience grows.

The Proper Use of Money

Luke 16:1–14 (following 2.7.2000)

'I tell you, use worldly wealth to gain friends for yourselves, so that when it is gone, you will be welcomed into eternal dwellings' (v. 9, NIV).

We continue with the unusual parable our Lord told concerning the dishonest or shrewd manager who, facing an enquiry into his stewardship, knew that, in all probability, he would be dishonourably discharged.

We assume that the rich man's manager had probably been robbing his master for a long time. When, however, he had to face his master, the manager, considering himself too weak for hard work and unsuitable for begging, thought of a plan which might rescue him from either. He therefore called in his master's debtors and reduced the amount of money they owed (*vv. 3–7*). Surprisingly to us, the master commended him, probably because he was himself capable of sharp practice (*v. 8b*) and although he was the victim he admired the servant's originality. We are left believing that the master would have employed similar tactics had he been in the same position. Even so, although he applauded his servant's actions, there is no suggestion that the master reinstated him.

Jesus was pointing out that the cheating servant *made money work for him*, because it provided him with friends who would help him. We must be clear on the fact that Jesus was not applauding his behaviour – far from it; but he was drawing attention to the fact that the people of this world are more shrewd than the people of light (*v. 8*). We, who are the children of light, can *make money work for us and for our Lord*. We can use our money to relieve poverty. We can sponsor, educate, help provide clinics and many other benefits which glorify God. We may or may not be known for our generosity, but we will be laying up treasure in heaven (*cf. Matt 6:19–21*). In righteous hands wealth can achieve much.

TO PONDER

> *Fading is the worldling's pleasure,*
> *All his boasted pomp and show;*
> *Solid joys and lasting treasure*
> *None but Zion's children know.*

(John Newton, SASB 157)

PRAYER SUBJECT   *Impoverished inner-city areas.*

The Testing of the Prophet (1)
1 Kings 13:7–10

> 'The king said to the man of God, "Come home with me and have something to eat, and I will give you a gift" ' (v. 7, NIV).

God had given very clear instructions to his man that while he was out on his mission he was not to eat, drink or even return home by the same route (*v. 9*). We do not know how far the man of God had travelled to reach Bethel. If he belonged to Jerusalem we are considering a round trip of some forty miles, but he may have lived much nearer to the border between the two kingdoms. Even so, any journey in a hot climate is demanding, and to do it without a drink was a costly requirement. Perhaps it was one of the ways in which God ensured that his prophet was mission-orientated. When, therefore, the king invited him home to share a meal the man of God had his answer ready.

There must have been many occasions where the strength of a divine command has been weakened by the messenger being compromised by hospitality and receiving gifts. King Jeroboam was to be left in no doubt concerning the non-negotiable nature of the message the man of God had brought. Hospitality and gifts, with the expressions of thanks which inevitably follow, were to give no comfort to the rebellious king. We can see, therefore, that in this command God was protecting his servant.

We wonder why the man of God was told to return to Judah by a route different from the one used to approach Bethel. If the reasons included the messenger's safety, the plan failed because soon the prophet was to drop his guard. He who had been unflinching before an angry king and resolute in his refusal of hospitality, yielded to the beguiling words of a member of the prophetic fraternity (*v. 18*). Is it fair to assume that God had to send a prophet from Judah to challenge Jeroboam because Israel's prophets had compromised themselves by not speaking out against the king? The man from Judah had not thought things through very well.

PRAYER

> Grant to me, Lord, consistency:
>   A heart both trusting and aware,
> A gentle, firm persistency,
>   That keeps me faithful everywhere.
> My will to follow you, Lord, reinforce,
> That I might run and finish well my course.

The Testing of the Prophet (2)
1 Kings 13:11–34 (11–22)

'Now there was a certain old prophet living in Bethel, whose sons came and told him all that the man of God had done there that day' (v. 11, NIV).

Thus far the man of God from Judah had done everything God had required of him. With great courage he had challenged King Jeroboam and with enormous faith had prophesied regarding the altar and interceded for the king (vv. 3–6). The prophet had obeyed the command not to eat or drink and resisted the king's invitation to dine, even though his body was probably in need of some kind of sustenance (v. 7). Obediently, the messenger chose another route for his way home and, well satisfied with the work he had done, rested in the shade of an oak tree before continuing with his journey (v. 14). Unfortunately, as he rested his body his spiritual defenses seemed to be at ease also.

At this point another prophet entered the arena. He was an old man of Bethel who had been told of the day's events by his sons (v. 11). It was a disastrous thought that made the old man wish to make contact with the Judean prophet. As we have suggested (WoL 10 July 2000), this prophet may well have been compromised by Jeroboam; indeed, he may have been a false prophet. Certainly, he was capable of lying (v. 18).

That the man of God should rest was not surprising. His day had been long, demanding and exhausting. Deprived of food and drink he would feel the need to rest for a while, but the fact that the old man was able to catch up with him seems to suggest that our man was dallying, and his sense of mission had weakened. Although he told the old prophet that he was not permitted to eat or drink, he accepted the old man's lie that God had given him a word which amended the original command (v. 18). The man of God should have realised that God would have told him personally if his orders were being changed. Temptation comes from many quarters – sometimes, alas, from within the community of faith.

PRAYER
> So often, God through other people speaks:
> His message comes in ways that he thinks best.
> And though our hearts another message seeks
> His word is truth made manifest.
> It is for us to weigh the words we hear
> And let the Spirit make the message clear.

The Testing of the Prophet (3)
1 Kings 13:20–34

'While they were sitting at the table, the word of the Lord came to the old prophet who had brought him back' (v. 20, NIV).

That the man of God succeeded in his primary task is clear but, because he listened to the lie of the older prophet, he failed in his overall mission. If he had only realised that his mission would not be complete until he had reached Judah. The story creates problems for us! Matthew Henry probably expressed a common viewpoint: 'The case was lamentable that so good a man, a prophet so faithful, and so bold in God's cause, should, for one offence, die as a criminal, while an old lying prophet lives at ease and an idolatrous prince [lives] in pomp and power.'

The historian, however, would have recorded this story because of the effect it had on the people of Judah, the southern kingdom, and as a lesson for future generations. It is not enough to be obedient to God up to a certain point only; total obedience is required.

We take note also of the fact that the lying prophet was capable of receiving a genuine word from God which he communicated to our much more attractive man of God (vv. 21,22). There are aspects to the death and burial of the man of God which help to modify our assessment of the story. His own people would read the favour of God in the fact that the lion, having killed him, did not devour him but, miraculously, stood by as though protecting the body from other creatures (v. 28). Furthermore, they would be impressed at the tribute paid by the old prophet when he insisted that on his own death he was to be buried in the same tomb as the man of God (v. 31). Later generations would be impressed also by the action of Josiah who, when he was purging the land of idolatry and burning the bones of pagan priests (v. 2), refused to disturb the bones of the brave prophet who had challenged Jeroboam (2 Kgs 23:15–18). Perhaps the man of God did not go unrewarded after all.

TO PONDER
Within a puzzling story we can see
Important lessons for our future good.
If we would represent him as we should,
We must obey his orders totally.
And when our frailty mars a glorious day,
God's mercy is not very far away.

An Inadequate view of God

1 Kings 14:1–20 (1–11)

'At that time Abijah son of Jeroboam became ill, and Jeroboam said to his wife, "Go, disguise yourself, so that you won't be recognised as the wife of Jeroboam. Then go to Shiloh. Ahijah the prophet is there"' (vv. 1,2a, NIV).

God is so great: his powers are beyond our comprehension and his moral attributes far exceed our ability to understand. It follows, therefore, that we all have an inadequate view of God; but some people seem to imagine that God is a person who can be manipulated or deceived. Jeroboam, who ought to have known so much better, falls into this category.

As our Scripture for today reveals, Jeroboam's son Abijah became ill. Clearly, the illness was of such severity that its treatment was beyond the skills of those who were usually at the king's disposal. In his distress Jeroboam turned for help to Ahijah, the prophet of the God he had disobeyed. In turning to Ahijah he thought he could deceive both the prophet and God and secure his information in that way. To Jeroboam, as with many other people, God is a person to turn to in times of extreme need. In this regard the king displayed the perversity of which many people are capable. God had promised Jeroboam a kingdom – 'all that your heart desires' on condition that he was faithful and obedient (*11:28–38*). With a promise of that quality behind him Jeroboam had no cause to fear the future either nationally or personally but because of his folly we find the historian telling this pitiful story of distress and attempted deception. As we would expect, Ahijah the prophet, once the bearer of good news to Jeroboam, was prompted by God to give the king the worst of bad news. Not only would his son die, but the kingdom, so generously given, would be taken away from him (*vv. 6–16*).

The massive sins of history are related to the fact that national leaders have an inadequate view of God. News headlines highlighting individual sins have the same cause as, indeed, do our own failures in obedience.

PRAYER   *Increase my understanding, Lord,*
                    Of your great love and holiness;
                    Your mighty grace and majesty,
                        Your wisdom and your righteousness.
                    And help me live my future days
                    As one who lives within your gaze.

A Shrewd Substitution

1 Kings 14:21–31

'In the fifth year of King Rehoboam, Shishak king of Egypt attacked Jerusalem. He carried off the treasures ... He took everything' (vv. 25,26, NIV).

Except for this episode in the life of Rehoboam, Solomon's son and King of Judah (12:1–25), it is not our intention to examine the lives of the kings of Israel and Judah as they make their sad marks in history. Rather, we will concentrate on the prophets whom God raised up to challenge the authority of so many of these evil men.

We note that Shishak, king of Egypt, conquered Jerusalem and robbed the temple and palace of their treasures. The historian makes much of the theft of the golden shields with which Solomon had equipped his guards. When Solomon, and then Rehoboam, moved between the palace and temple, the guards must have looked magnificent as they held their shields of pure gold. Rehoboam must have been devastated by the overall loss of wealth, but the loss of the golden shields was too public and humiliating a loss for him to endure. Shrewdly, he had a new set of shields made out of bronze (v. 27). Although not as splendid as the golden shields, in time, because burnished bronze would flash in the sunlight almost as well as gold, few would notice the difference.

This substitution of bronze for gold is symbolic of what had happened to the people of God, and that can still happen today. As the baser metal became an acceptable substitute for the purest gold, so the pure worship which was at the heart of Israel was substituted by acts of worship which were decidedly inferior. Truth gave way to falsehood and only the responsible and discerning would notice the substitution. Sadly, people can be satisfied with substitutes. Formalism replaces faith; planning, although important, needs divine guidance; activity should be born of prayer: substitutions are so easy to make. An enemy can steal the originals from us and we can so easily not notice or be concerned.

PRAYER
Make pure my heart, O Lord;
Make me both strong and resolute
To hear and to obey your word,
Accept no other substitute.
Let not my foolish, undiscerning eyes
Be pleased with bronze when pure gold is the prize.

Ahab and Jezebel
1 Kings 16:29–34

'In the thirty-eighth year of Asa king of Judah, Ahab son of Omri became king of Israel, and he reigned in Samaria over Israel for twenty-two years' (v. 29, NIV).

The kingdoms of Israel and Judah, those two confusing strands of Hebrew history, continued to run their slow and sad course of almost unrelieved evil (*see 15:9–24*). Conditions in the northern kingdom worsened with the accession of Ahab (*vv. 30,33*), becoming even more evil following his marriage to Jezebel (*v. 31b*). So evil was Ahab that the historian said that he 'considered it trivial to commit the sins of Jeroboam' (*v. 31a*). God, however, had not deserted his people and was to provide a witness for himself in the person of Elijah the prophet.

Ahab was vulnerable because he was a weak rather than a strong man. He was open to manipulation and in his wife Jezebel resided all the powers of evil necessary to influence him into ways which merited the historian's harshest judgments. Jezebel's background was the worship of Baal, a fertility god whose devotees were often involved in the most degrading behaviour. Once she became Ahab's queen, Jezebel's mission was to spread Baal worship. Such was the power of her personality that she succeeded in influencing life in both Israel and Judah to an enormous degree. Even after Ahab's death she continued her evil ways and her dramatic death suggests that time had not minimised her capacity for evil (*2 Kgs 9:30–37*).

King Solomon merited the judgment of God because he tolerated the pagan worship of his wives (*11:1–11*), but Ahab sinned so much more than Solomon because he built altars to Baal and then worshipped him (*v. 31*). In this story of the life of Ahab we see how tolerance of evil leads on to actual sin; and in the life of Jezebel we see how powerfully one person can influence another. More than that, we see how one person can affect great numbers of people, even nations.

PRAYER

Make my heart sensitive to hear
*   The footsteps of approaching sin.*
Grant to me, Lord, a holy fear,
*   Lest in my life sin enters in.*
Make my defences strong and sure,
And keep my faith in you secure.

A Poor, Rich Man
Luke 16:19–31

'There was a rich man who was dressed in purple and fine linen and lived in luxury every day' (v. 19, NIV).

This parable about the rich man and the beggar who sat at his gate could so easily be a continuation of the previous parable about the shrewd manager. Our Lord's comment there, 'use worldly wealth to gain friends for yourselves, so that when it is gone, you will be welcomed into eternal dwellings' (*v. 9*), is appropriate here. We take note of the emphasis Jesus placed upon the man's wealth. He did not say, 'a rich and generous man' or a 'rich and honourable man': clearly, our Lord intended us to conclude that the rich man was that, and only that. He loved money and consequently did not love God (*v. 13; cf. v. 14*).

Jesus chose the name of the beggar with some care. Lazarus means 'God is my help'; it could be argued that God had not helped him much but Jesus was drawing a picture of two contrasting people, one luxuriously rich and the other painfully poor. We could conclude that since extreme poverty often gives rise to envy, resentment and bitterness, God had helped Lazarus because, in due time, the comforts of heaven were his. Even in death the contrast was drawn between the two: the rich man was buried and Lazarus was just disposed of as a person of no worth.

To illustrate our Lord's statement that 'What is highly valued among men is detestable in God's sight' (*v. 15b*), Jesus had the position of the two men reversed after death. The man who in life was only rich became the poor man suffering the divine judgment, and Lazarus, the righteous poor man, was at Abraham's side. The rich man still seemed to believe that Lazarus was at his disposal (*vv. 24,27*) but Jesus was making two things clear. First, our place in eternity depends on the kind of life lived on earth and second, discipleship is based, not on that kind of miracle (*vv. 27,28*), but on our response to the revelations God has already given.

PRAYER
> *In quietness of heart and mind,*
> *By depth of thought and act of will,*
> *I choose your better way to find,*
> *And in my life your plans fulfil.*

PRAYER SUBJECT *Cities which have high unemployment.*

Born to Greatness
1 Kings 17:1–7

'Now Elijah the Tishbite, who was of the settlers of Gilead, said to Ahab, "As the Lord, the God of Israel, lives, before whom I stand, surely there shall be neither dew nor rain these years, except by my word" ' (v. 1, NASB).

In this almost continuous record of national evil, another man of God suddenly appeared. Of his background we know little except that he came from Tishbe on the eastern side of the river Jordan. It is assumed that he was a member of a school of prophets where he learned to become aware of God and how to become a prophet (*cf. 2 Kgs 2:5; 4:38*).

Elijah is one of the great figures in the Old Testament. Anyone doubting that claim has only to read the last two verses in the Old Testament which declare that God will send Elijah again to earth (*Mal 4:4–6*), and the fact that our Lord identified that coming with the person and ministry of John the Baptist (*Matt 11:11–15*). Of significance also is the fact that at the Mount of Transfiguration Jesus was joined by Moses and Elijah (*Matt 17:1–3*). Honours come no greater than that.

As we have noticed, prophets were men of courage who did not hesitate to place themselves in danger (*13:1*) but thus far no prophet had challenged enemies more fearsome than Jezebel and Ahab. As he faced Ahab, Elijah gave the reason for his courage, 'As the Lord, the God of Israel lives, *before whom I stand*' (*v. 1b*): more important than merely standing in front of the king, Elijah stood before the living God. As God was real to Elijah in the helpful context of the school of prophets, so God was real to him as he stood before Ahab. But that was not all. As Elijah stood before God so, even though he did not know it, Ahab stood before God; the difference being that Elijah stood before a God of infinite mercy and Ahab stood before God of absolute judgment. It was the making of Elijah and the undoing of Ahab. In all our trials and difficulties we, too, stand before God. What an encouraging fact that is!

PRAYER   *Wherever I may be I stand before you, Lord,*
         Your grace encircles me and living is your word.
     Though foes are hard to face with weapons close to hand,
         Sufficient is your grace when in your will I stand.
     Cast out my natural fear, let me be confident,
         Remind me that you are the Lord omnipotent.

A Promised Drought
1 Kings 17:1–7

'As the Lord, the God of Israel lives, before whom I stand, surely there shall be neither dew nor rain these years, except by my word' (v. 1b, NASB).

Drought has always been a devastating experience for people. Even today, with all our skills in locating underground supplies of water, and ability to extract the water, drought turns fertile lands into deserts and causes people to leave their districts in search of food. Although the drought was God's punishment on Ahab and Jezebel, its effects would be felt by all people. The historian does not state the exact duration of the drought (*cf. 18:1*) but our Lord said that it lasted for three and a half years (*Luke 4:25; cf. Jas 5:17*). It was a terrible judgment on king and people in response to their rebellion and the persistent sin of idolatry.

Of particular interest in this prophecy of an extended drought is the fact that Baal was the god of fertility. In Canaanite thought, Baal was the spirit of life in the earth, the one who enabled animals and people to procreate, and *who was the god of life-giving rain*. Given that explanation, it follows that if Elijah, the prophet of Israel's living God, could dry up the heavens and prevent crops from growing, then Baal, the god of Ahab and Jezebel, was a weak or false god and only Israel's God was powerful and real. The prophecy of Elijah, therefore, was a challenge of enormous significance to everyone caught up in Baal worship (*cf. 18:21b*).

From Elijah's prophecy of a drought affecting the land we proceed to the idea of the drought which affects the soul, and conclude that there is a drought wherever people refuse to acknowledge God. Under those conditions there is a dearth of spiritual joy and depth of contentment, but carelessness and evil thrive. Hearts are parched because of the absence of living water; vital proof that Jesus alone can end the drought.

PRAYER

O disclose thy lovely face!
Quicken all my drooping powers;
Gasps my fainting soul for grace
As a thirsty land for showers.
Haste, my Lord, no more delay;
Come, my Saviour, come away.

(*Charles Wesley, SASB 412*)

Marching Orders
1 Kings 17:1–7

'Then the word of the LORD came to Elijah: Leave here, turn eastward and hide in the Kerith Ravine, east of the Jordan' (vv. 2,3, NIV).

This simple statement in the story of Elijah implies so much. It appears as though when God ordered Elijah to confront Ahab he did so without giving Elijah any idea concerning what would happen next – and Elijah had faith enough to obey without asking questions. We would possibly have been plying God with a question or two such as: 'What next, Lord?' 'When I have delivered your word am I to stand there until Ahab makes me a prisoner and punishes me for my prophecy?' Not so Elijah! He was prepared to move with God one step at a time. If that was God's plan, the prophet could accept it. Having delivered his prophecy God gave specific instructions concerning Elijah's hiding place. Because Kerith, like Gilead, was east of the Jordan (*v. 1*), we wonder whether the brook was known to him. It was a narrow gorge or ravine created by the torrents which had coursed down to the Jordan through the centuries.

Kerith, although intended by God as a temporary haven for Elijah from the wrath of Ahab and Jezebel, was much more than mere shelter. During this time, his faith in God and trust in his providence were strengthened. He must have learned also to value some of the lesser birds in creation. Had we been making this kind of provision for a prophet we would have used eagles, not ravens; but God had a better plan. No observer would have queried the descent of ravens into the ravine (*v. 6*), but they would have noted the presence of a more majestic bird. To the Hebrews, a raven was unclean (*Lev 11:13–15*), it was a scavenging bird fit only to be driven away – but it was valuable to God and to Elijah.

Many of us can recall a humble place where God has rested and reinforced us and where we have been spiritually fed by unlikely people. God sometimes surprises us with the messengers he sends to us.

PRAYER   *O Lord, you come to us in many ways:*
A brook like Kerith proves a hiding place,
Its food and shelter signs of endless grace.
How often you have moved my heart to praise!
Continue, Lord, my faith to reinforce,
And keep my soul upon its rightful course.

An Alien Land
1 Kings 17:8–16

'Then the word of the LORD came to him: "Go at once to Zarephath of Sidon and stay there. I have commanded a widow in that place to supply you with food" ' (vv. 8,9, NIV).

As the drought continued to afflict the land even the brook, Kerith, dried up and it was time for Elijah to move on. Remarkably, of all the locations God had at his disposal in which to hide the prophet, he chose Zarephath, where a widow woman had been prepared to provide him with food. A glance at a map of the area reveals the surprising fact that Zarephath was not a nearby village. To reach it Elijah was involved in a journey across Israel of some one hundred miles because Zarephath was in Phoenicia: a pagan and hostile country. We must assume that this town offered more safety to Elijah than any town in Israel and, like Elijah, we must conclude that God knew what was best for him.

We note that God had commanded a widow woman to provide for Elijah (*v. 9*). The command had interesting consequences. So far was she from having her own well-stocked larder, that she was resigned to death by starvation, and that of her son also (*v. 12*). It appears that the preparation God had made resulted in the woman being willing to share her last scrap of food with the man of God. As though God was testing the widow's faith further, he had Elijah ask that she should first make him a small cake and then prepare food for herself and her son (*v. 13*). To make the widow more confident, Elijah gave her the promise God had given him that 'The jar of flour will not be used up and the jug of oil will not run dry until the day the Lord gives rain on the land' (*v. 14*). That the woman accepted this promise speaks much of her trust, especially since she was a pagan: 'As surely as the LORD *your* God lives' (*v. 12a*) seems to confirm her non-Hebrew background. Clearly, there was much more to this widow-woman than was at first apparent; not least that she was capable of exercising a profound selflessness of heart and simplicity of trust in Elijah and his God. She has much to teach us.

PRAYER   *I would be much more trusting, Lord,*
                    Of selfishness be drained.
              I would more closely hear your word,
                    In faithfulness be trained.
              My faith and love, O Lord, renew,
              To dominate the things I do.

A Pause for Reflection

1 Kings 17:1–16

'Elijah said to her, "Don't be afraid ... For this is what the LORD, the God of Israel, says" ' (vv. 13a,14a, NIV).

We can hardly avoid observing the simplicity of Elijah's faith. Although he was a man of great influence and spiritual stature, he was content to let the Lord lead him step by step and day by day. He seemed not to worry about the consequences of being thrust into difficult circumstances by God. When, for instance, he confronted the despotic Ahab, he remained untroubled by the existence or otherwise of an escape route. It was sufficient for him to trust God for his continuing deliverance. Ahab and Jezebel may have been formidable enemies, but their power and influence paled before that of Elijah's God.

The divine providence did not fail and God's next word to Elijah was 'Leave here, turn eastward and hide in the Kerith Ravine' (*v. 3*). Elijah's shelter from Ahab was assured and, although his fare fails to excite our taste-buds, it was regular and sufficient. More importantly, it was a twice-daily reminder of God's care of him (*v. 6*). Again came the command, 'Go at once to Zarephath of Sidon and stay there' (*v. 9*). Elijah obeyed and the record shows no trace of complaint or question. He neither argued nor made other proposals, being willing to do whatever God required of him. What strength there must be in that kind of obedience!

As the prophet arrived at the gate of Zarephath there, by God's providential ordering, was the very woman who had been commanded to feed him (*v. 10*). In those days, if a widow had no family to look after her she was condemned to a life of extreme poverty, and God had commanded such a person to care for Elijah. The situation cried out for a miracle and God was more than equal to the situation. The supply of flour and oil never failed (*v. 16*). God performed another miracle by allowing Elijah to bring the widow's dead son back to life (*vv. 17–24*).

PRAYER

> Let me follow you, O Lord,
> Step by step and day by day.
> Keep my life in full accord
> As I tread my pilgrim way.
> Build my faith and influence
> Through your gracious providence.

A Foot in Both Camps
1 Kings 18:1–15

'After a long time, in the third year, the word of the LORD came to Elijah: "Go and present yourself to Ahab, and I will send rain on the land" ' (v. 1, NIV).

It was time for another confrontation with the king and God gave the prophet the necessary command, 'Go and present yourself to Ahab' (v. 1). With customary obedience Elijah made his way from Zarephath to Samaria, observing that, if the drought had been harsh in Phoenicia, it had been even more severe in Samaria (v. 2). It is at this point in the story that we are introduced to Obadiah, a trusted official in Ahab's employment but also described as a 'devout believer in the Lord' (v. 3).

The one hundred prophets who had been hidden from Ahab by Obadiah, and fed by him, must have been glad of his high position in the palace (v. 4): but Obadiah's presence there raises questions. How, for instance, can a man be so agreeable to people like Ahab and Jezebel and, at the same time, be faithful to the Lord? Was Obadiah so compliant to the royal couple that they were unaware of his true feelings? How compromised was he, and did he ever implement some of Ahab's policies? We quite understand that if Obadiah used his position to affirm his faith in God he would have been killed (vv. 9,14) but secret discipleship of this nature poses problems. Our Lord's words, 'By their fruit you will recognise them' (Matt 7:16) seem to suggest that goodness cannot be hidden, and in Ahab's court where evil was the norm, goodness would be very conspicuous. Although the historian witnesses to Obadiah's faith and loyalty (vv. 12,16), he remains an enigma to us.

What vigilance Obadiah would have to exercise in order to avoid revealing his true feelings to Ahab and Jezebel! Should he have exposed himself to such spiritual danger? Would he have been wiser to have become one of the hunted rather than remain the confidant of the hunter? How glad we are we did not have to make Obadiah's decision!

PRAYER
Not always, Lord, are judgments easily made;
Should we take this way, or another tread?
How much we need your wisdom and your aid
Lest by our fears or wants we are misled.
Grant us, O Lord, to seek and know your mind
That life's sure path our hearts may always find.

The Nature of Faith

Luke 17:1–6

'The apostles said to the Lord, "Increase our faith!" ' (v. 5, NIV).

We can understand the disciples being challenged constantly in the presence of Jesus. His faith and deeds were in a different class from theirs and it would be natural for them to say to him, 'Increase our faith.' For them, the problem had become more acute because he had spoken with them about the need for a forgiving spirit, even for someone who sinned against them as many as 'seven times in a day' (*v. 4*). Of this, William Manson said, 'The requirement of a forgivingness which knows no limit seems to the apostles impractical, and they indicate their doubt by saying, "Give us more faith!" ' (*JM*). We would make the same request.

Implicit in the plea for more faith was an expectation that Jesus could supply it and, by the request, the disciples showed they were beginning to understand their Master's remarkable powers. They were not asking wrongly or of the wrong person but, arising from a growing awareness of his role, were making a practical prayer. If they were going to be his heralds (*cf. 10:1–24*), they needed more faith, or a better quality faith, than they possessed. They knew also that the faith they needed could not be self-generated; it had to come from a divine source (*Eph 2:8*).

The same awareness surges through our hearts from time to time. Because we know our hearts so well, we know that apart from Jesus we can do nothing (*John 15:5b*) and our faith and subsequent fruitfulness depend on our total reliance on our Lord. He has great plans for us (*John 14:12*) and we have great hopes (*cf. 9:57; 18:18; 24:21*), but those plans and hope will never be properly realised until his kind of faith is born within us. On our part the situation calls for desire, openness, obedience and the willingness to receive; our Lord will do the rest.

PRAYER

> To thee our humble hearts aspire,
> And ask the gift unspeakable;
> Increase in us the kindled fire,
> In us the work of faith fulfil.

(*Charles Wesley*)

PRAYER SUBJECT   *Field workers with relief organisations.*

A Strange Priority
1 Kings 18:1–15

'Ahab had said to Obadiah, "Go through the land to all the springs and valleys. Maybe we can find some grass to keep the horses and mules alive so we will not have to kill any of our animals" ' (v. 5, NIV).

Ahab's mindset is so very difficult for us to understand. His major concern appears to be for the welfare of his horses and mules. It seemed nothing to him that his people were suffering enormous privations because of his defiance of God, but his animals must not be allowed to suffer. We do not know why Ahab chose Obadiah to scour the countryside with him. Indeed, we do not know why Ahab went himself instead of delegating this task to others. Perhaps he felt he could not trust other people to share his concern for the animals above that for people. If that supposition is true, it shows how completely Ahab trusted Obadiah. On the other hand, this may simply have been the way in which God engineered the meeting between the evil king and the righteous prophet.

As he looked for fresh pastures for his king's horses, Obadiah met Elijah, recognised him immediately and received a message that terrified him: Elijah ordered him to 'tell your master' that 'Elijah is here' (v. 8). Obadiah knew his royal master far better than the prophet knew him, hence his fear. If he, Obadiah, told Ahab that Elijah was present, and the Spirit of the Lord moved Elijah elsewhere so that he could not be found, Ahab would kill him (vv. 8–14). Elijah reassured the fearful Obadiah who then sought out the king and gave him Elijah's message (v. 16).

In our imaginations we see these two men, Obadiah and Elijah, as they met on that dramatic day. Obadiah was fearful for his life even as he pleaded his faithfulness towards God (vv. 12b–14). In his faithfulness to God, however, Elijah looked forward to the confrontation with Ahab because he knew that God would not allow him to fail. Together, the two men display the difference between compromise and conviction.

PRAYER
Let me, O Lord, be strong,
And slow to compromise.
Let me know right from wrong,
See life through your pure eyes.
Give me the courage that I need
And boldness show in thought and deed.

Troublemakers

1 Kings 18:16–18

'So Obadiah went to meet Ahab and told him, and Ahab went to meet Elijah. When he saw Elijah, he said to him, "Is that you, you troubler of Israel?" ' (vv. 16,17, NIV).

If a ruler could be more concerned about his horses and mules than about his people (*v. 5*), we can see how easily he could regard Elijah as the 'troubler of Israel'. With such perverted values Ahab was capable of making irrational judgments but in one sense he was right about the prophet. It *was* Elijah who had declared there would be a drought in the land and that this would continue until he heard further from God.

It is common for people not to see themselves as the architects of their own difficulties. They blame this person or that, this set of circumstances or the other – sometimes they blame God. They then continue to live in their accustomed way. Not at any time did it seem to cross Ahab's mind that his god, Baal, had failed. As we have noted (*WoL 18 July 2000*), Baal was supposed to be the god of fertility and life-giving rain. The parched nature of the land and the scarcity of crops witnessed to either the helplessness of Baal or his unconcern; but Ahab continued to worship his impotent gods and blamed Elijah for the problem.

The Hebrew word which is translated 'trouble' has, like our English word, various shades of meaning. We can use it of a minor disturbance or inconvenience, or of something related to years of misunderstanding and violence within a country. Neither Ahab nor Elijah used the word in a trivial sense: both were referring to a disaster that for one or other of them could only become worse – much worse. With truth on his side, Elijah denied his role as a troublemaker; instead he identified Ahab and his family as the culprits. It was because of their disobedience to God and idolatry that disaster had befallen them (*v. 18*). Elijah, as God's appointed man, was now to lead the nation back into the old paths.

PRAYER

> *O for a heart both pure and strong,*
> *That lets me see with clarity*
> *The issues of both right and wrong,*
> *Then speak with power and charity.*
> *Lord, help me each new day discern*
> *The ways you choose, the ways you spurn.*

The Challenge
1 Kings 18:19,20

'Now summon the people from all over Israel to meet me on Mount Carmel. And bring the four hundred and fifty prophets of Baal and the four hundred prophets of Asherah, who eat at Jezebel's table' (v. 19, NIV).

The blindness and folly of the ungodly heart are perfectly illustrated by the way in which Ahab accepted Elijah's challenge. Instead of using his authority to punish Elijah for the trouble he had caused and his presumption in giving orders, Ahab agreed to do as he was told. The drought, and the impotence of his gods, ought to have persuaded Ahab that a contest between Baal and God could have but one outcome but blind, stubborn and foolish, he made the arrangements Elijah asked for.

From the moment the challenge was issued to the crowd assembled on Mount Carmel many days must have passed by. We imagine Jezebel, Ahab and the priests of Baal building up their collective confidence in success; and we visualise Elijah seeking the counsels of God in prayer and faith. The prophet knew how much was at stake. He knew also that the God who had authorised the drought, and taken care of him at Kerith and Zarephath (*17:1–24*), would not allow him to fail.

Elijah's faith and courage were outstanding. Although it was incorrect of him to say, 'I am the only one of the Lord's prophets left' (*v. 22; cf. 19:18*), he knew nothing of seven thousand others and believed himself a lone witness. To stand against Ahab and Jezebel, the pagan priests and an idolatrous nation, required conviction of the highest order. Ever since then, God's people have been encouraged by the prophet's holy boldness. Our Lord's brother James made a statement which should encourage us even more, 'Elijah was a man just like us' (*Jas 5:17a*). *Just* like us? Does that mean that we who are quite ordinary Christians can have the same qualities of faith and boldness? It is part of the glory of the gospel that we can answer that question in the affirmative.

PRAYER

I sink in life's alarms
When by myself I stand;
Imprison me within thine arms
And strong shall be my hand.

(George Matheson, SASB 508)

Truth and Certainty
1 Kings 18:20–29

'Elijah went before the people and said, "How long will you waver between two opinions? If the LORD is God, follow him; but if Baal is God, follow him" ' (v. 21, NIV).

On the day when the multitude assembled on Mount Carmel the atmosphere must have been alive with excitement and not a little apprehension. This was more than mythology's 'War of the Titans'; it was a war 'against the rulers of the darkness of this world, against spiritual wickedness in high places' (*Eph 6:12 AV*) and many would feel the importance of it. Most who had gathered were tainted by idolatry, and Elijah's heroic stand for God had put them on the defensive. The prophet's question, 'How long will you waver between two opinions?' was calculated both to challenge and to make it possible for them to return to God. In addition, the simple statement, 'If the Lord is God, follow him; but if Baal is God, follow him' would appeal to them as reasonable and fair.

Like the indecisive people they were, the Israelites wavered in their allegiances. One day they favoured Baal; another day they favoured the Lord. On the one hand they followed the king in his worship and the degrading desires of their hearts with their debasing satisfactions; on the other hand, they moved towards the worship of the true God who required obedience, love, morality, and who offered a life of fulfilment.

In a sense, the situation Elijah faced is one which confronts us today. A large percentage of people claim to believe in God and turn to him in times of great stress or fear but, much of the time, they worship at the world's shrines of power, wealth and indulgence. The prophet's challenge, therefore, is relevant. Baal, however, is not God. Baal represents the universal need of mankind to worship but is a false god because he is shaped in the image of man. How important it is that we who belong to God act as beacons lighting the way of a hesitant world to his feet!

PRAYER

Though men have wrought confusion
Thy hand still holds the plan,
And thou, at length, decideth
The destiny of man.

(Albert Dalziel, SASB 6)

The Contest Begins
1 Kings 18:22–29

'Then you call on the name of your god, and I will call on the name of the LORD. The god who answers by fire – he is God' (v. 24a, NIV).

As we read the dramatic account of the contest between the prophet of the Lord and the prophets of Baal, we savour every detail, because we know that, in reality, it was no contest at all. Baal was defeated long before his prophets prepared the bull for sacrifice; but the people did not know that and if Baal's prophets had any doubts they concealed them well. The Israelites entered into the spirit of the contest because when Elijah said, 'The god who answers by fire – he is God', they answered, 'What you say is good' (v. 24b). Elijah's challenge was clear and fair.

With great pleasure the historian recorded the antics of the prophets of Baal as they pleaded for a positive response from their god. Hour after exhausting hour they pleaded and danced around the altar. At noon, so the account runs, Elijah began to taunt them, 'Shout louder . . . perhaps he is deep in thought, or busy, or travelling. Maybe he is sleeping and must be awakened' (v. 27). Spurred on by Elijah's goading, the prophets of Baal began to cut themselves with swords and spears until they were awash with their own blood (v. 28). Their frenzy was a powerful witness to their devotion to Baal but it availed nothing. From noon 'until the time for the evening sacrifice' (v. 29b), that is 3 p.m., these devotees of the god Baal continued with their pleading.

When it was clear that Baal had failed in the challenge to demonstrate that he was God (v. 29c), Elijah took centre stage again. He had complete confidence in God's willingness and ability to answer him by fire. We assume that in those quiet hours of prayer afforded him while Ahab organised the gathering on Carmel, God had given Elijah the assurance of victory he needed. He could afford, therefore, to spend time heightening the drama because a momentous miracle was about to take place.

PRAYER

God knows our heart's most dominant desire,
But answers prayer according to his will.
He had decreed he would respond with fire
When bold Elijah stood on Carmel's hill.
It is for us to pray, and let God choose
How different situations he will use.

Faith and Obedience
1 Kings 18:30–39

'Then Elijah said to all the people, "Come here to me." They came to him and he repaired the altar of the LORD, which was in ruins' (v. 30, NIV).

The failure of the prophets of Baal gave Elijah the opportunity for which he had been waiting. No miracle of fire could follow the frenzied pleadings of the prophets of a false god and, on their proven failure, Elijah stepped forward, faced the people and asked them to 'Come here to me'. As they moved forward, drawn by his authority, they did not realise they were being drawn also to Elijah's God. It is not unusual for God to give his representatives this role and influence. Often, when people draw close to a godly person, they become aware of a spiritual dimension which can, in time, lead them to a knowledge of our heavenly Father.

Thoughtfully, and with a deep awareness of the significance of his actions, Elijah rebuilt the altar of the Lord using twelve stones, one for each of the tribes. It would not be lost on the people that the prophet included the two tribes belonging to Judah in this important ritual. He then began to make things more difficult for himself. Instead of allowing the wood used in the sacrifice to be tinder-dry, he had a trench dug around the altar and quantities of water poured over the sacrifice, the wood and the altar so that everything was saturated; as the prophet expected, the trench filled with water. The crowd, which included the discredited prophets of Baal, could see that no tricks were being employed: if the fire came, it had to be genuine fire, strong enough to turn wet wood into a fire and fierce enough to consume the sacrifice.

After Elijah had prayed – to which prayer we will return (*WoL 3–5 Aug 2000*) – the miracle happened. The flames dried the water-filled trench, burned the sodden wood, and the bull was sacrificed to God. Having answered by fire there could be no doubt – the Lord was God (*v. 24b*).

PRAISE

> *All ye who own his power, proclaim*
> *Aloud the wondrous story,*
> *Cast each false idol from his throne,*
> *The Lord is God and he alone:*
> *To God all praise and glory!*

(Johann Jakob Schutz, trs Frances Elizabeth Cox)

SUNDAY 30 JULY

A Pause for Thought
Luke 17:5,6 (following 23.7.2000)

'The apostles said to the Lord, "Increase our faith!" ' (v. 5, NIV).

As we meditate further on this simple request which the disciples made of
Jesus, we realise that the request was made as a group, 'Increase *our* faith'.
The earnest individual plea, 'Increase our [my] faith' was lodged firmly in
the corporate prayer and this personal element must never be overlooked or
minimised. Even so, we all together stand in great need of a richer, deeper,
more effective faith in our Lord, and the community element in this prayer
will be overlooked to our mutual impoverishment.

As the people of God we need a better-quality faith than we possess. The
cliché is true of the Church, the congregation, and the Christian group, that
the sum of the whole is greater than the sum of its individual parts. When we
come together our interactions with each other should enliven our faith,
making it more adventurous, visionary and practical. As we meet, needs
within the congregation should be perceived, as should be the needs of the
community in which we worship. And it is the community we are called to
serve. Our corporate faith needs to be increased to ensure that our witness in
the locality might flourish. Because we want to meet real and felt needs our
faith will result in meaningful initiatives and the development of programmes
consistent with local resources. From these initiatives we would expect that
some of the new people being served will eventually become disciples of our
Lord.

Faith affects our relationship with God, how we approach the Scriptures,
our prayer life; indeed, everything we think of or do. To sum up: the prayer
'Lord, increase our faith' should ensure that the ongoing work of the Spirit
within us as individuals will be maintained, and that our work as the body of
Christ in the community will prosper.

PRAYER

Help us to build each other up,
Our little stock improve;
Increase our faith, confirm our hope,
And perfect us in love.

(*Charles Wesley, SASB 662*)

PRAYER SUBJECT   *Christian witness in the community.*

The Cost of Idolatry

1 Kings 18:40–42a

'Then Elijah commanded them, "Seize the prophets of Baal. Don't let anyone get away!" ' (v. 40a, NIV).

Ahab and Jezebel had wrought havoc in the land because of their idolatry. The establishment of Baal worship as standard practice in Israel was a terrible sin which had undermined the will of the people to worship the true God. Because of the nature of Baal worship, the morality of Israel had sunk to the lowest depths; idolatry, therefore, had exacted a high price from the people. In time, Ahab and Jezebel would suffer their punishment but the priests, who had plied their trade so effectively, were to be punished immediately. To our twenty-first-century eyes there is something barbaric about the slaughter of these men, but we are not to measure Elijah's actions by our culture: *then* was different from *now*.

It was because of the success of the priests of Baal and Asherah (*v. 19b*) that the country had gone astray. Ahab, Jezebel and the priests had wooed the people from worshipping God and, in consequence, the drought had come. If the priests had been left alive, they would have been a cancerous growth within the body of the nation, and the future required that the growth should be removed; hence their deaths. We note that the people, who were the victims of the idolatrous priests' success, turned on the men who had exploited and demeaned them (*v. 40b*), and gave their loyalty to the true God because of the miracle of fire.

King Ahab was unable to help his priests as the people first captured and then slew them. When Elijah told him to 'Go, eat and drink', Ahab did so like a man traumatised and without protest (*vv. 41a,42a*). How could he eat and drink when his god had been overthrown and all his prophets lay dead? Perhaps Ahab felt that his day of revenge would come and Elijah would pay a high price for it! But the victory over Baalism that day meant that Elijah could 'hear the sound of a heavy rain' (*v. 41b*).

PRAYER
Life has its sure rewards:
The fruit of sin is death,
But those who are the Lord's
Are filled with living breath.
O Lord of grace and purity
Let your love's fruit be seen in me.

Another Step in Faith
1 Kings 18:41–46

'So Ahab went off to eat and drink, but Elijah climbed to the top of Carmel, bent down to the ground and put his face between his knees' (v. 42, NIV).

After the slaughter of the priests (*v. 40*), Ahab, the king who had shown more concern for his horses than his people (*v. 5*), retired to his tent for a meal, but Elijah needed to pray. The prophet knew that his task would not be completed until the rains came, the parched land was soaked and the streams and gullies gurgled with running water. Elijah, therefore, went to the top of Mount Carmel and bowed before the Lord.

We see this man who, had he been self-orientated, could have stood before God requiring that he should honour his word and send the rain; instead, he 'bent down to the ground and put his face between his knees'. Elijah's posture revealed his sense of awe at God's power, his total dependence on him, his gratitude for the victory over idolatry, and his deep humility. The prophet knew that this victory was due entirely to God and that he was but an instrument in God's hands. Even so, as he worshipped he worked. Almost always, faith is work. It is the defeat of doubt, the subjugation of the inner life to the will of God and the conquest of evil. In this instance, since the sky was cloudless, Elijah's faith was being stretched even further. His task was, as yet, unfinished.

The historian does not tell us much about Elijah's prayer, but we make the obvious deduction that it was expectant and persistent. Seven times the prophet sent his servant to scan the skies over the sea for evidence of a rain-cloud. When after the seventh time the servant reported a cloud 'as small as a man's hand is rising from the sea' (*v. 44*), Elijah's faith told him that, small as the cloud was, it was big with the promise of God. In this particular instance on Mount Carmel we perceive a general rule of the spiritual life: namely, that our heavenly Father has a wonderful way of using our limited but sincere faith to achieve his great ends.

PRAISE

> *Faith, mighty faith, the promise sees*
> *And looks to that alone;*
> *Laughs at impossibilities*
> *And cries: It shall be done!*

(*Charles Wesley, SASB chorus 118*)

Triumph

1 Kings 18:44–46

'So Elijah said, "Go and tell Ahab, 'Hitch up your chariot and go down before the rain stops you' " ' (v. 44b, NIV).

With all the confidence of a prayer-reinforced faith, Elijah told the servant who had observed the small cloud over the sea to go to Ahab, and tell him to return home before the deluge made the roads impassable. Remarkably, Ahab acted upon the prophet's word. As an ungodly man, Ahab could have been expected to look at the clear sky and conclude that Elijah was wrong, but the events of the last hours had modified his judgment. As a pagan, he could not accept Israel's God, but he was prepared to give God's man the benefit of any doubt at this time.

It seems incredible that Elijah should run before Ahab's speedy chariot to Jezreel – a distance of some eighteen miles. Were it not for the power of the Lord (*v. 46a*) the feat would have been impossible, but it was an important thing to do. Among other beliefs, Baal-worshippers believed their god 'was the god who rode on the clouds, the god who understood lightning, and the god who set his thunder-bolt in the heavens' (*A. Graeme Auld*). Had the king ridden at the head of his entourage some witnesses might have assumed that Baal had triumphed. With Elijah at the head, however, it was clear evidence that the living God had honoured his word and the rains had come in blesséd consequence.

We visualise the scene: the darkest of clouds, the heaviest of rain, the man of God, hair streaming in the high wind, drenched by the rain, and racing ahead of the furious, defeated Ahab. The king would want to talk with Jezebel, his superior in intelligence and malevolence, who would tell him what next to do. Elijah would know, of course, that the defeat of Baal, and this near-marathon run were but a prelude to further action.

PRAYER

O man of God, run well today,
Empowered by God, mark Ahab's way!
Be sure that when this drought has passed
The powers of evil will be massed
Against you, make your heart afraid:
But God is near to give you aid
And, weak and fearful though you be,
His power will give you victory.

The Prophet's Prayer (1)

1 Kings 18:36–38

'At the time of sacrifice, the prophet Elijah stepped forward and prayed: "O LORD, God of Abraham, Isaac and Israel, let it be known today that you are God in Israel" ' (v. 36, NIV).

It was in the morning that the prophets of Baal commenced their sacrifice in the hope that Baal would answer them by fire (*v. 26*). At noon Elijah taunted them and from then until late afternoon they pursued their frenzied prayers until they were exhausted. It was at the time of sacrifice – that is, the time laid down when Israel's sacrifice in the temple was to be made. Even the timing of the sacrifice on this dramatic day spoke of the continuity of worship to Israel's God throughout the centuries.

The historical link was further reinforced by the opening words of Elijah's prayer: 'O LORD, God of Abraham, Isaac and Israel'. The idolatrous Israelites were being reminded that God, the living God, had called their forefather from a pagan land to found the nation of which they were a part (*Gen 12:1*). The less-colourful Isaac was an important link in their faith, and Jacob, renamed Israel (*Gen 32:28*), stands out as one of the great figures in their history. From Jacob, Israel was to take its name.

By his prayer, Elijah was asserting the faithfulness of the living God to Israel throughout the generations. He is a God who hears prayer. Unlike the priests of Baal, who pleaded, danced and even bled to attract their god's attention, Elijah only had to address God in faith for proof that God was real. To Elijah, God was the supreme reality of life, and he was confident God would hear and respond.

PRAYER

> O God of Bethel, by whose hand
> Thy people still are fed,
> Who through this weary pilgrimage
> Hast all our fathers led;
>
> Our vows, our prayers, we now present
> Before thy throne of grace;
> God of our fathers, be the God
> Of their succeeding race.

(*Philip Doddridge, SASB 918*)

The Prophet's Prayer (2)
1 Kings 18:36–38

'At the time of sacrifice, the prophet Elijah stepped forward and prayed: "O LORD, God of Abraham, Isaac and Israel, let it be known today that you are God in Israel and that I am your servant and have done all these things at your command"' (v. 36, NIV).

Every step taken by Elijah was ordered by God. It was God who told him to confront Ahab, to hide at Kerith, move to Zarephath and then to present himself, yet again, to Ahab (*17:1–9; 18:1*). Not one of these initiatives had been generated by Elijah. Common sense could suggest to us that since God was the initiator and source of power it would not be necessary for Elijah to pray asking God to 'let it be known today that you are God in Israel'. The record shows plainly that such a revelation was God's intention. But life in the Spirit does not always follow the pattern of common sense. The divine wisdom far exceeds ours.

God does not give his promises to us in order that we will reduce the frequency or force of our prayers. Were he to do that, we would know him less rather than more, and that would be a massive deprivation for us. The promises God gives are actually meant to draw us closer to him. They are intended to make us more in tune with him, and bring to the fulfilment of his plans our own faith which, mysteriously, is an essential ingredient to any successful spiritual venture. God was counting on his prophet's obedience and faith. We *are* instruments in God's hands, but we are *more* than that: we are 'God's fellow-workers' (*1 Cor 3:9a*).

Out of the lovely simplicity of his inner life with God, Elijah prayed that everyone might know that he was God's servant, and that all he had done thus far was at God's command. The prophet was not strutting on a large stage but was pointing the Israelites, the priests of Baal, and the king himself away from disobedience to God: the God who gives life and to whom everyone is accountable. What great obedience Elijah had!

PRAYER

> *My God, my Father, make me strong,*
> *When tasks of life seem hard and long,*
> *To greet them with this triumph-song:*
> *Thy will be done.*

(Frederick Mann, SASB 744)

The Prophet's Prayer (3)
1 Kings 18:36–38

'Answer me, O LORD, answer me, so these people will know that you, O LORD, are God, and that you are turning their hearts back again' (v. 37, NIV).

As we meditate further on the prayer of Elijah we are impressed by the fact that it was so God-centred. The only personal qualities of Elijah which come through relate to his servanthood and obedience. There is a total absence of self-consciousness and this must be due to his absorption in his task and awareness of his place in the Lord's plan. Elijah did not posture because he had an impressive audience of leaders and people; he remained a servant, addressing the God who was his master.

The prophet had two major concerns, the first of which was the glory of God; hence the simple prayer, 'Answer me, so these people will know that you, O Lord, are God.' It pained Elijah that the living God who had covenanted himself with Israel had been betrayed by king and people as they flocked to worship Baal – a god made by human hands and sometimes worshipped in a most degrading fashion (*cf. 14:24*).

Elijah's second main concern was that his people should know God and return to him. The prophet knew his people's heritage and, having a deep personal knowledge of God, desired that the Israelites should forsake their sin and live like the people God had chosen to be his own.

We note also that God honours prayer. God chose not to emphasise his sovereignty by acting independently of his prophet. The record makes it clear that when the prayer was concluded, '*Then* the fire of the Lord fell' (*vv. 37,38*). In honouring the prayer, God honoured Elijah in front of the people. That massive congregation would not be thinking of theological niceties at that time; their perception was that the prophet prayed, and in response to that prayer the fire came. God honoured both the petition and the petitioner, as so often he does.

PRAYER
You are so kind and loving, Lord,
* You honour those who honour you.*
All those who take you at your word
* Can see your hand in all they do.*
How much you love! How much you bless
All who in love your love express!

A Perspective on Rewards

Luke 17:5–10 (following 30.7.2000)

'Suppose one of you had a servant ploughing or looking after the sheep. Would he say to the servant when he comes in from the field, "Come along now and sit down to eat?" ' (v. 7, NIV).

The idea that we should be rewarded for good work is common to most of us. Even if there is no material reward, at least there should be appreciation. As a leader of unsurpassed quality, Jesus must have been constantly encouraging his disciples and spurring them on to greater things. When, for example, they had returned earlier from their great mission, they were greeted by a Christ who was full of gratitude, first to God and second to his disciples. After his prayer of thanksgiving our Lord turned to the disciples and said, 'Blessed are the eyes that see what you see' (*10:23*); what a reward that must have been for each of them!

Our chosen parable is difficult insofar as it focuses on the work of a servant – more accurately, a slave – who, after he has worked outside all day, returned to his master's house, there to learn that he must prepare his master's meal before he could eat himself. The disciples might have been surprised to hear the gracious Christ saying, 'Would he [the master] thank the servant because he did what he was told to do?' Our Lord continued, 'So you also, when you have done everything . . . should say, "We are unworthy servants; we have only done our duty." ' (*vv. 9,10*).

Following the parable of faith and the mustard seed, our Lord seemed to be saying that faith, great faith, is the norm and should be expected of each follower. Great rewards there are as we well know, but our service should be done without such expectation. Edward A. Armstrong suggests that 'the faithful servant is one whose life is a joyful offering of work and service'. Each day we strive to do more to please our Master.

PRAYER

It is my duty my best work to do,
To serve you as my Saviour and my Lord:
To be a good ambassador for you,
And seek no recognition or reward.
What satisfaction, Lord, your service gives,
Now that your Holy Spirit in me lives!

PRAYER SUBJECT   *Hospice patients and their staff.*

Jesus and Seven Disciples
John 21:1–3

'Afterwards Jesus appeared again to his disciples, by the Sea of Tiberias. It happened this way' (v. 1, NIV).

From the dynamic certainties of Elijah facing Ahab, we turn to seven disciples of our Lord who, at this time, seemed to be very uncertain, 'at a loose end', as we sometimes say. We can account for their presence in Galilee (*Matt 28:7*) but we have a little difficulty with the mindset that made fishing seem to be a natural thing to do. They had passed through the trauma of our Lord's death to the exaltation of his resurrection. Jesus had met with them in the Upper Room, had breathed his Spirit on them and commissioned them for service (*20:21–23*) but, at this time in Galilee, they do not impress us as men with a deep sense of mission.

It has been suggested that, mission or not, they still had to eat, and fishing was their best way of making a living. An impression given by the scriptural account is that they were reverting to their former way of living because it gave them comfort and security, and this has a strong element of probability in it. The great events recorded in the previous chapter (*20:1ff.*) do not seem to be motivating them. Peter said, therefore, 'I'm going out to fish' and the other six said, 'We'll go with you' (*v. 3*). As they had done so many times before, they got into the boat, launched it out into the sea and commenced to fish.

William Temple interprets Peter's statement, 'I'm going out to fish' as an indication of self-will, and the agreement of the other disciples as a willing identification with Peter's self-determination. It was an innocent enough exercise in its own right, but it was self-chosen. Night-time was always the best time for fishing and they would expect a large catch, but they caught nothing. Archbishop Temple deduced therefore that, 'the work which we do at the impulse of our own wills is futile'. Had not Jesus said to them earlier, 'apart from me you can do nothing' (*15:5b*)?

PRAYER　　　　*When I pursue my own, self-chosen way,*
　　　　　　　　　Believing that my strength can generate
　　　　　　　Success sufficient to fulfil each day,
　　　　　　　　　And my life's dream to consummate;
　　　　　　　Then will I find in ways which cause me pain
　　　　　　　That without Christ, my life is lived in vain.

The Caring Christ
John 21:4–6

'Early in the morning, Jesus stood on the shore, but the disciples did not realise that it was Jesus' (v. 4, NIV).

As we have assumed, the disciples were uncertain and seemingly without a strong sense of mission, but that could not be said of their Master. In his love he continued to be with them, pastor them, and point them to their destiny. Even though they were unaware of him, he was wonderfully aware of them: he would not let them go. Reading beneath the surface of John's account we see that in the darkest night, in the most discouraging and frustrating situation, Jesus is never very far from his disciples and, in his own positive way, offers assistance. Would it not be true also to affirm that, even when we do not recognise him because we think it is someone else speaking, his word can come to us with helpful clarity? More than once in our lives we have been able to say to another person, 'Your word has been the word of the Lord to me today!'

We note that as the frustrated disciples approached the shore, Jesus called out to them. Scholars emphasise that Jesus addressed them (*v. 5*) using a word which has nuances difficult to translate into English. 'Friends' is favoured by the NIV and NEB, whereas the NASB chooses 'children'. James Moffatt translated the word as 'lads' and the Good News Bible opted for 'young men'. The greeting was warm and affectionate. It was also authoritative. When the stranger told them to cast their net on the right side of the boat they obeyed without question, and the net was filled with fish immediately (*v. 6*). Having pointed out that 'work which we do at the impulse of our own wills is futile' (*WoL 7 Aug 2000*), William Temple commented further, 'What is done in obedience to the Lord's command, even though he who gives the command is not recognised, results in overwhelming success.' Our hearts agree with Temple's remarks. Metaphorically, our nets have been empty when self-effort has motivated us, but overflowing when we have been obedient.

PRAYER

> *Our Lord is never far away,*
> *   The darkest night to him is day,*
> *And as our problems he beholds,*
> *   His plan for us in love unfolds.*
> *If we obey his blest commands,*
> *Then full will be our hearts and hands.*

Recognition
John 21:7–14

'Then the disciple whom Jesus loved said to Peter, "It is the Lord!" ' (v. 7a, NIV).

If, as we imagine, John – the disciple whom Jesus loved – was more finely tuned to the mind of Christ than was Peter, we are not surprised that John recognised Jesus first. Who but Jesus would be able to perform a miracle of that magnitude (vv. 6,11) and who but Jesus would be there when his disciples most needed him?

It was typical of Peter that, when he realised who the stranger was, he should cast a cloak around himself, plunge into the water and make his way towards the Master (v. 7b). On a previous occasion he had done this, and when he looked at the wind-tossed seas on which he had cast himself, he began to sink (Matt 14:29,30). This time there was no such hazard and Peter reached the shore in safety. The six remaining disciples struggled with the catch which was so heavy that they were unable to haul it aboard. They used the buoyancy of the water to take the weight and towed the net to the shore (v. 8). It was at this point that they observed the preparation Jesus had made for their return and heard him say, 'Bring some of the fish you have just caught' (v. 10). The energetic Peter returned to the boat, dragged the net on land, opened it and 153 fish tumbled out on to the beach.

Scholars tell us that many attempts have been made to read significance into this figure of 153. With imagination and ingenuity, if not success, dedicated men have tried to make the number yield its secret. The more pragmatic William Temple wrote, 'It is perverse to seek a hidden meaning in the number; it is recorded because it was found to be the number when the count was made. Yet *the net did not break*.' Temple continued, 'The gift of God is always more than we can receive yet it never bursts the vessel which we can offer for its reception.' Perhaps we ought to let that simple explanation inspire and challenge us.

PRAYER

*Because you are the Christ, your mighty power
Can make provision for our every need.
In times of stress, in failure's testing hour,
Your love initiates a kindly deed.
If only we were more in tune with you
We would see more of you in all you do!*

A Meal Provided

John 21:7–14

'When they landed, they saw a fire of burning coals there with fish on it, and some bread' (v. 9, NIV).

To a group of tired and frustrated men, the knowledge that Jesus was with them must have been wonderfully energising; but the sight of that fire and the smell of that fish cooking must have lifted their spirits immeasurably. How like Jesus to make such practical provision for them!

The writer wants us to deduce that the amount of fish being cooked was insufficient to feed all of them, hence the invitation, 'Bring some of the fish you have just caught' (*v.10*). The problem, if it was that, was by Christ's design. If by miraculous means he could produce fish, he could have produced enough for a complete meal. Clearly, Jesus was reinforcing the concept of partnership with his disciples: the meal would be complete only when they had made their contribution. We take note of the fact that the bread, which they could not at that time produce, was supplied fully by the Master.

By virtue of their power, God and his Christ could do everything required to advance the gospel, but by virtue of their strategy, it was essential that the disciples, indeed, all disciples, should make their own contribution. Whatever resources or gifts we have, they are needed by our Lord. As Paul so wisely observed, 'We are God's fellow-workers' (*1 Cor 3:9a*). Even so, when we consider the manner in which the disciples acquired the fish they were able to bring to the breakfast meal, we realise that whatever it is we are able to give has come from our Lord in the first place. We have no resources, gifts or abilities that have not come from him, but he builds our self-esteem by not reminding us of that fact. 'Bring some of the fish you have just caught' remains his approach.

PRAISE
> *He works by invitation, not by force,*
>   *He never seems to overrule the will;*
> *'Bring of your fish': most gently said, of course,*
>   *'Put them with mine, this waiting dish to fill.'*
> *He could have made the meal all on his own,*
>   *But this way, he could build their self-esteem.*
> *The meal was theirs, and not from him alone:*
>   *Love works that way, and love must rule supreme.*

A Gracious Host
John 21:7–14

'Jesus said to them, "Come and have breakfast" ' (v. 12a, NIV).

The net had been dragged to the beach, its contents spread out by the amazed disciples as they counted 153 fish and noted that they were large fish (*v. 11b*)! Can we imagine their feelings? Weary after a long night's work they had been commanded to cast their net at the right side of the boat and the resultant catch was too heavy to handle. The stranger had been identified as Jesus, their risen Master, with them for the third time since his resurrection (*v. 14*), and it seems as though the miracle of the catch and the unexpected presence of the Lord were more than they could handle. When he said to them, 'Come and have breakfast' they held back. More than that; although they knew it was the Lord, 'None of the disciples *dared* ask him, "Who are you" ' (*v. 12b*).

Why would they not dare to ask him? Was it because the experience was too good to be true and they feared the question might prove that they were dreaming or hallucinating? Or were they overwhelmed with awe at the sight of the Risen Christ, and moved by reverence and wonder that the eternal world had broken in upon them in the form and presence of the crucified Lord? In those circumstances we would not have been any more bold, and Jesus, knowing their feelings, gave them a simple invitation, 'Come and have breakfast'. As their reticence continued, Jesus took some of the food he had prepared, moved towards them and offered it (*v. 13*). The barrier disappeared and we are left to assume that the Master and his seven disciples finished the cooking and shared the meal. Neither before nor since has there been a breakfast like this. The disciples knew they were not dreaming and knew also that if their sense of mission had weakened (*WoL 7 Aug 2000*), this breakfast was calculated to bring it into sharp focus again. The Master was with his men, their fellowship was renewed and reassuring, and the scene was set for them to learn some important lessons about the way ahead.

PRAYER
> To you, O Lord, we dare to come:
> We dare – because it is your will;
> We dare – because your work is done,
> And Calvary's deed we must fulfil.
> We dare – because our hopes and needs are great,
> And your love, Lord, our hopes will consummate.

SATURDAY 12 AUGUST

The Reinstatement of Peter
John 21:15–17

'When they had finished eating, Jesus said to Simon Peter, "Simon son of John, do you truly love me more than these?" ' (v. 15a, NIV).

The disciples' tiredness must have disappeared as they shared the meal with Jesus. Nearby on the beach lay the evidence of a highly successful catch, and in their hearts was the exaltation of Easter Day. Christ was risen, and the future of his chosen disciples glowed with resurrection glory. Jesus, however, had a special work to do in the heart of Simon Peter; he who had but recently said, 'I will lay down my life for you' (*13:37b*) and who even more recently had said of Jesus, 'I don't know the man' (*Matt 26:72*). In all, he denied his Lord three times. Now, at the lakeside Jesus was to challenge him three times.

After the meal the group would be much more relaxed and, with the conditions exactly right for a healing work to be done, Jesus led with the question, 'Simon . . . do you truly love me more than these?' Although it could be argued that 'these' refers to Peter's role as a fisherman, many scholars believe that 'these' are the other disciples. In support of this, we note that when Peter was called by Jesus to be a disciple he was not following his trade as a fisherman (*1:41*). Furthermore, the other disciples were fishermen and our Lord did not bother to address them in this vein and it would have been as relevant to them as to Peter. But Peter had always been in the forefront. He had perceived the divinity of Christ before the others (*Matt 16:16*); had affirmed his loyalty in absolute terms (*13:37b; Mark 14:29*); had drawn his sword to defend Jesus when the others held back in Gethsemane (*18:10*); and while the others were in hiding, had gone with John to the High Priest's house (*18:15*). We assume, therefore, that our Lord's question could be restated as, 'Simon, son of John, do you truly love me more than your fellow-disciples love me?' It would have been a big challenge to make had Jesus been alone with Peter, but the challenge was greater because other disciples were present.

PRAYER
My heart is slow, Lord, to compete
With others in my love for you;
Make my frail heart with love complete,
Revealing love in all I do.
To love you well, Lord, is my heart's desire,
Then with your love set my poor heart on fire.

A Parable about Prayer

Luke 18:1–8

'Then Jesus told his disciples a parable to show them that they should always pray and not give up' (v. 1, NIV).

Once again our Lord encouraged the disciples to pray (*cf. 11:5; Matt 7:7*); he knew how vital the discipline of prayer is, and we are persuaded also that prayer is essential. As William Cowper wrote (*SASB 646*):

> *Restraining prayer, we cease to fight;*
> *Prayer makes the soldiers' armour bright;*
> *And Satan trembles when he sees*
> *The weakest saint upon his knees.*

Persistence – or importunity – in prayer is important also. We do not know why some prayers seem to take a long time before they are answered, but experience teaches us that not every prayer is granted immediately. We have to hold on in faith and in the process our faith is tested and strengthened while our hearts are kept tender and faithful.

Jesus proceeded to tell the parable of an unjust judge who 'neither feared God nor cared about men' (*v. 2*) and who would not listen to a widow's plea for justice. Widows fared badly in those days and, in addition to the usual disregard, it is probable that this one lacked the money to bribe the judge. Believing in her cause and having no money the widow came back, day after day, to demand justice (*v. 3*). Not because her case was just, but because her persistence had given her a nuisance value the unjust judge heard her. We do not even know whether her cause was just – not all persistent people have right on their side – but the judge was prepared to award her the case. If an unjust judge can reward persistency, how much more generous will be our righteous heavenly Father?

PRAISE   *Thou art coming to a King,*
       Large petitions with thee bring,
       For his grace and power are such
       None can ever ask too much.

            (*John Newton, SASB 563*)

PRAYER SUBJECT   *For more use of prayer as a means of grace.*

A Problem of Translation
John 21:15–17

'Jesus said to Simon Peter, "Simon, son of John, do you truly love me more than these?" "Yes, Lord," he said, "you know that I love you"' (v. 15b, NIV).

The Greek word lying behind the word 'love' which Jesus used in his question is different from the Greek word which lies behind the word 'love' in Peter's response. The love of which Jesus spoke is of a higher order than the much more ordinary word for love which Peter used. In an attempt to mark the difference between the two 'loves' the NIV translated our Lord's use as 'truly love me'. It is significant that our Lord's question and Peter's answer were repeated (v. 16), but on the third occasion, our Lord changed his word to the one Peter had used, hence the dropping of the qualifying word 'truly'. The change hurt Peter's feelings and he replied with some warmth; even so, he did not use the love-word which indicated the higher form of love.

B.F. Westcott makes the perceptive comment that 'the foundation of the apostolic office is laid in love and not in belief'. In its truest form, love presupposes belief as Paul indicated so beautifully (*1 Cor 13:1ff*).

In his answer Peter affirmed his love for Jesus but, as we have observed, did so on a lower level. To this Jesus replied with a command, 'Feed my lambs' (v. 15b). Peter's role was being changed from that of a fisherman to a shepherd and in this, the first stage of his commissioning, he was given responsibility for the young. In those early days of the Church when the young, in any society, were required to respect older people, that may well have been a simple, almost trivial task; but in our prevailing culture it is a task of enormous complexity and stress. The importance of shepherding the young in Christian ways cannot be overestimated. Although caring for the lambs is very close to the great Shepherd's heart, today it remains both difficult and costly. Notwithstanding the difficulties, however, it is a command the Church must not ignore.

TO PONDER

There's a world at random drifting,
Which belongs to Christ the Lord:
He is claiming youth's allegiance
Till his Kingdom is restored.

(Will J. Brand, SASB 868)

The Second Question
John 21:16

'Again Jesus said, "Simon son of John, do you truly love me?" He answered, "Yes, Lord, you know that I love you." Jesus said, "Take care of my sheep" ' (v. 16, NIV).

We imagine a pause following our Lord's command to Peter, 'Feed my lambs' (*v. 15b*). During that time Peter would be assessing the command in order to determine its significance for him. No doubt also the other six listening disciples would be thinking of the implications of the task given to Peter and wondering whether it would affect them. After the pause, Jesus repeated the question but, this time, he omitted the three words 'more than these' (*v. 15a*). He was no longer making a comparison between Peter and his colleagues.

Presumably, Jesus spoke in the same measured tones as before and Peter, puzzled, wary perhaps and not knowing quite what to say, repeated his first reply (*v. 16*). This time the Lord responded with, 'Take care of my sheep'. The verb 'to care' had, and has, enormous implications. Such care – tending – has to do with the whole person. It is the provision of food but it includes also guiding, counselling, encouraging and nurturing. In fact, it was to mean demonstrating the same shepherding qualities our Lord himself possessed and displayed.

We assume that by nature Peter was not a natural carer. As a born leader he was inclined to be at the front and possibly knew little of what was going on behind. His was a thrusting, eager, needing-to-be-first personality (*cf. v.7; Matt 14:28,29*). As people gathered around Jesus we imagine Peter being in the front rank and as close to the Master as possible. It was left to Philip and Andrew to be in the background and, in consequence, more accessible to the crowd (*12:20–22*). The fisherman was to become a shepherd, the leader was to add the attributes of the shepherd to his remit, and care for the flock was required of him.

PRAISE

If we truly love the Lord,
*   We will take him at his word.*
As he cared, so we will care,
*   Other people's burdens share.*
By our actions glorify
Christ, for whom we live and die.

The Third Question
John 21:17

'The third time he said to him, "Simon son of John, do you love me?" '
(v. 17a, NIV).

Three times Simon Peter denied his Lord (*18:15–18,25–27*) and three times Jesus asked him to reaffirm his love. This had great meaning for Peter, of course, but it was of considerable importance to the other six disciples because it was part of Peter's rehabilitation with them also. Although they followed him on this fishing trip (*v. 3*), his real authority stood in need of reinforcement. That more than half of the disciple-group were witnesses to Peter's commissioning was crucial to everyone.

As we have already observed (*WoL 14 Aug 2000*), in his third question Jesus did not use the word that represented the higher form of love; rather, he used the word with which Peter had responded to him. The NIV marks this change by omitting the adverb 'truly' (*cf. vv. 15,16 with v. 17*). We assume that Peter was hurt because Jesus had felt it necessary to remind him of his threefold denial, the pain and shame of which he continued to feel; hurt also because Jesus even seemed to be questioning his love at the lower level of regard when perhaps Peter, because of his recent past, had felt that he could not use the more exalted, generous and purer word for love.

We cannot help but feel that Jesus would have been happy to receive from Peter that nobler word. No one needs schooling less in the weaknesses of men and women than Jesus. He who bore the world's sin on the cross knows the nature and weight of human transgressions. But he values the aspirations of the human heart also. He knows the importance of setting standards which are beyond our reach because his Spirit is able to make us measure up to them. If we aim for a humanly unachievable target we will reach a higher level than if we aimed only for the humanly possible mark. Sadly, Peter's modesty was modifying his aspirations.

PRAYER

> O help me, Lord, to aim
> For levels higher than my reach.
> My unadventurous spirit teach
> The love and power I can claim.
> Let but my earthbound soul aspire,
> And I can live as you desire.

Peter's Appeal
John 21:17

'He said, "Lord, you know all things; you know that I love you" ' (v. 17, NIV).

To our Lord's third question, Peter responded more with his heart, exclaiming with great vigour, 'Lord, you know all things; you know that I love you.' They were the words Peter needed to say and that the other disciples needed to hear. It was a whole-hearted response that cleared the way for our Lord to complete Peter's restoration and commissioning.

Peter was right – of course the Lord knew all things. From the beginning Peter's heart had been an open book which the Lord read accurately. When Andrew first brought his brother Simon to Jesus, our Lord looked at him and said, 'You are Simon . . . You will be called Cephas' (*1:40–42*). As the NIV footnote says, 'Both Cephas (Aramaic) and Peter (Greek) mean *rock*.' Jesus understood that behind Peter's impulsiveness and frailty was the heart of a loyal, faithful man. Although our Lord rebuked him (*13:6–11; Matt 16:21–23*), he never rejected him. Even though Peter denied the Lord (*Luke 22:54–62*), indeed, *because* he had denied him, after his resurrection Jesus sought Peter out and revealed himself as the Risen Christ. That was not the action of a Saviour who did not know the mind and heart of his disciple. He knew Peter's frailty, but he knew also Peter's strengths and potential. Our Lord's ability to forgive, restore and recommission a failed disciple is quite wonderful, and is an enormous encouragement to us as we struggle with our weaknesses.

PRAISE

Of course he knows!
Does he not have the eyes to see
Deep in the heart of you and me?
Does he not read there all our needs,
The thoughts that motivate our deeds?
*   He knows – and to us kindness shows.*

Of course he knows!
He is the Christ, our Saviour, Friend,
His love is real and cannot end.
Had he not known our sin and guilt
Redeeming blood could not be spilt.
*   He knows – and mercy overflows.*

Ownership

John 21:17

'Jesus said, "Feed my sheep" ' (v. 17b, NIV).

For the third time Jesus followed Peter's protestation of love with a command. First, he was told, 'Feed my lambs' (*v. 15b*); second, he was told to 'Take care of my sheep' (*v. 16*); and third, he was told to 'Feed my sheep' (*v. 17b*). Of these commands W.E. Vine wrote, 'In the spiritual care of God's children, the feeding of the flock from the word of God is the constant and regular necessity; it is to have the foremost place. The tending (which includes this) consists of other acts of discipline, authority, restoration, material assistance of individuals, but they are incidental in comparison with the feeding.'

Common to each of the commands is the possessive adjective 'my'. The flock does not belong to Peter or any other leader – it belongs to God; he owns the flock – he owns us. We often wonder why he treasures us so much but have to marvel at the greatness of his grace. What a comfort it is to know that we belong to God and know that he will not lightly cast us aside! It is almost breathtaking to remember that just as God said, 'This is *my* Son, whom I love' (*Matt 3:17*), Jesus said to Peter, 'Feed *my* sheep.'

Those whose ministry is one of feeding God's sheep know that an enormous responsibility has been laid upon them. The task, surely, has to be approached with an awareness of the importance of their role in God's strategy. With the diligence of the good shepherd who seeks the best pasture for his flock, so must the preacher, teacher or pastor discharge their responsibility. The green pastures are there to find.

It is, however, a tremendous privilege and a great, unsought honour to be entrusted with this task of sharing insights from the word of God. Whoever fulfils this role is crucial to the ongoing work of redemption and is richly blessed by God in return.

PRAISE
We are a blest possession of the Lord:
To his choice flock by grace we are restored.
Though to inconstancy we still are prone,
The Lord our God regards us as his own.
What comfort and what hope of future bliss
That God should love us with a love like this!

The Command Obeyed

1 Peter 5:1–11

'To the elders among you, I appeal as a fellow-elder, a witness of Christ's sufferings and one who also will share in the glory to be revealed: Be shepherds of God's flock that is under your care, serving as overseers' (vv. 1,2a, NIV).

Some thirty years after he had received his commission from Jesus (*John 21:15–17*), Peter was proving how faithfully he had accepted the Lord's lakeside commands. As an itinerant apostle he had visited the churches in Asia minor and, because of the trials they were currently experiencing (*1:6*), wrote to encourage them in order that they might stand firm in the faith. The 'painful trial' to which he refers (*4:12*) is translated as the 'fiery ordeal' in NASB, NEB, REB and JBP; some commentators think this might refer to the persecution under Nero when Christians were martyred in the most cruel of ways.

A quick reading of this letter will indicate just how tenderly, skilfully and responsibly Peter shepherded these new Christians, some of whom were converted Jews (*1:1*) and some of whom were pagans (*2:12; 4:3,4*). The apostle made the Old Testament very relevant to them and made it very clear how Jesus had fulfilled the ancient Scriptures (*2:6–10*).

Our chosen Scripture, however, shows how completely Peter had internalised the concept of the shepherd and how clearly he understood its importance. Leaders were to be shepherds also. Leaders are to be shepherds, not because they have a need to dominate (*vv. 2b,3*) but because they have been called to serve (*v. 2c*). It would appear as though elders received some form of remuneration; payment, however, was not to be a motive for service but a due recognition of their eagerness to serve (*v. 2d*). Peter's appointment as a shepherd and his observations of the life and ministry of Jesus had made him aware of the fact that shepherding, at every level of ministry, was to be the norm. Were it not so, he would not have described our Lord as the 'Chief Shepherd' (*v. 4a*).

TO PONDER   *The shepherd-heart is one the Christ bestows*
Through whom alone we know true charity;
And by his Spirit love within us grows
To help us serve without disparity.
To one another we must show his care,
With one another all his treasures share.

Another Interpretation
Luke 18:1–8 (following 13.8.2000)

'And will not God bring about justice for his chosen ones, who cry out to him day and night? Will he keep putting them off? I tell you, he will see that they get justice, and quickly' (vv. 7,8a, NIV).

Just as many expositors, with much justification, point out that this parable teaches the value of persistence in prayer (*WoL 13 Aug 2000*), there are others who believe that the main lesson taught by the parable is that God will not unduly delay his response to earnest prayer. This is not to say that importunate prayer is not a necessity, but it is to say that God does not delay his answers without good reason.

This alternative deduction from the parable has its basis in the fact that Jesus is not *comparing* God with the unjust judge; on the contrary, Jesus is *contrasting* one with the other. All that the unjust judge is, God is not. The judge procrastinated because he was careless (*v. 2*) and probably corrupt. He yielded to the widow because she was pestering him and, obviously, would continue to do so. As a careless, corrupt and unaccountable judge, he was willing to give her justice as she perceived it, to free himself from her demands. God is not like that at all. Jesus made it clear that God will bring about justice – as he sees justice – for his people. He will not keep putting us off because he loves us and loves righteousness and, as Jesus said, 'he will see that they get justice, and quickly' (*v. 8a*).

The command that we 'should always pray and not give up' (*v. 1b*) is of great importance to us. For some people, some circumstances and some events we will petition God for years, whereas other prayers will be answered immediately. The prayers are ours; the answers are in God's hands. According to his wisdom, his reading of circumstances and the hearts of people, our Father-God will respond without unnecessary delay.

PRAYER

Here may we prove the power of prayer
To strengthen faith and sweeten care,
To teach our faint desires to rise,
And bring all Heaven before our eyes.

(*William Cowper, SASB 604*)

PRAYER SUBJECT   *For more 'schools of prayer' to be established.*

The Consequence of Love
John 21:18,19

'Jesus said ... "I tell you the truth ... when you are old you will stretch out your hands" ' (vv. 17b,18a, NIV).

What excitement, joy and fulfilment the future held for Peter because of his love for Jesus! He was to be filled with the Holy Spirit and preach the Christian Church's first sermon – a sermon that resulted in three thousand becoming believers immediately (*Acts 2:1–41*). He was to heal a crippled beggar at the temple gate (*Acts 3:6*); be arrested by the Jewish authorities (*Acts 4:3*); be led by the Spirit to open the kingdom's doors to the Gentiles (*Acts 10:1ff.*); and be imprisoned and released by an angel's hand (*Acts 12:1ff.*). Those were heady days for the disciples.

As the more recently-made apostle, Paul grew in influence as evangelist, church planter, pastor, and theologian, Peter's role in the Church became less clear, but there can be no doubt he was active and fruitful in his activity (*1 Cor 1:12* [NB, 'I follow Cephas']). Again, in defence of his own apostleship, Paul referred to the 'other apostles and the Lord's brothers and Cephas' (*1 Cor 9:5*) who, quite obviously, moved around the churches inspiring and nurturing them. We can imagine the pleasure with which the scattered groups of Christians received Peter and how they would receive his words with pleasure. We imagine also the kind of questions they might ask him about Jesus, about his interview with the Risen Christ (*Luke 24:34*), and his lakeside commissioning (*vv. 15–17*).

The people would not need to ask what was meant by 'when you are old you will stretch out your hands' (*v. 18a*) because that was a euphemism for crucifixion. In Peter's case, his love for Jesus was to mean martyrdom on a cross. For thirty long, influential and fruitful years, Peter knew that his privilege would be to share the same kind of death as his Lord, *and it seemed not to have been a burden to him* (*1 Pet 1:7; 2:20–24; 4: 12–19*). He knew enough about his Lord to trust him for the future.

TO PONDER

> *A consequence of love is joy,*
> *   And fruitfulness and influence;*
> *To know and prove the Master's peace,*
> *   Because with love comes confidence.*
> *If love should end in sacrifice,*
> *True love will not refuse that price.*

The Last Command
John 21:18–23

'Then he said to him, "Follow me!" ' (v. 19b, NIV)

It is of interest to observe that the last command Jesus gave to Peter, 'Follow me', corresponded with the first command he gave when he called both Peter and his brother Andrew from their nets: 'Come, follow me' (*Matt 4:19*). Then, of course, they were told they would become 'fishers of men' whereas now Peter the fisherman was to be Peter the shepherd. Following is a very personal business insofar as Jesus calls us *as we are* to become disciples. Time, however, does not weaken the need to follow; indeed, quite the reverse. Furthermore, experience teaches us that as we develop our skills and become richer in spirit, following Jesus becomes even more satisfying because we follow more thoughtfully and fruitfully.

In Peter's case, he was to follow Jesus to the cross itself (*vv. 18,19*). Not everyone is called to die for Christ. But Peter could not resist asking the Lord what would happen to John (*v. 21*) and received the reply that the pattern of John's discipleship was no concern of Peter (*v. 22*). The way in which Jesus couched his reply to Peter gave rise to the belief that John would not die but, obviously, people made the wrong assumption (*v. 23*). The fact is clear that just as we become believers on an individual basis so our discipleship continues to be distinctive, even though we are all members of the body of Christ.

God does not mass-produce or clone his disciples. There is a richness about our personalities which the Holy Spirit wishes to refine, reinforce and use in the Master's business. Consequently, there is an important place in the body of Christ for all kinds of gifts and potentiality. Peter was not John, and neither of them was Paul, but each had his own distinctive contribution to make to the building up of the Church. Our individuality ought not to make us difficult, proud and self-indulgent, but rather should make us part of the rich mosaic of the people of God.

PRAYER
We know, Lord, we are wonderfully made,
We differ in both gifts and personality.
But with your Holy Spirit's powerful aid
His wisdom and originality,
Within Christ's body we can take our place,
And witness to your all-sufficient grace.

The Limitless Christ
John 21:24,25

'Jesus did many other things as well. If every one of them were written down, I suppose that even the whole world would not have room for the books that would be written' (v. 25, NIV).

On reading the Gospels it soon becomes evident that the writers have been selective in their use of events and elements of our Lord's teaching. Not one of the four evangelists aimed at saying everything they knew about Jesus: the task would have been too great and, furthermore, would not have served the purpose for which he wrote. This final sentence in John's Gospel is not mere exaggeration as its face value suggests. Rather, it is hyperbole – that is, an exaggerated statement not meant to be taken literally. Our world is not too large to contain all the *books* that could be written about Jesus, but it is certainly not large enough to contain *him*. Although the deeds of Jesus could have been noted and his teaching collated, the significance of his deeds and teaching is incalculable.

Early in his ministry Jesus described himself as the gate or door (*10:9*) and we, who have moved into the Father's sheepfold through him, have discovered that we have become citizens of an eternal kingdom, with the resources of his eternal world in all its wonder and glory to be sampled here and enjoyed to the full hereafter. The magnitude of that life is hinted at in Scripture but its true nature is beyond our imaginings.

How can we, for example, begin to understand what union with Jesus means? Or what it means to share the Lord's resurrection life or be a joint-heir with Christ (*cf. Eph 2:6; Col 3:1; Rom 8:17*)? We let the great truths of Scripture and experience roll around our minds and are enriched by the process, but only a small fraction of their worth is assimilated. Christ is so much bigger than we think: he offers us so much and we take so little; even so, his love continues to flow and his Spirit continues to encourage and challenge us. He is, truly, a limitless Christ.

PRAISE

> *This, this is the God we adore,*
> *Our faithful, unchangeable friend,*
> *Whose love is as great as his power,*
> *And knows neither measure nor end.*
>
> (*Joseph Hart, SASB 962*)

The Gospel of Mark
Mark 1:1–3

'The beginning of the gospel about Jesus Christ, the Son of God' (v. 1, NIV).

The Gospel which bears Mark's name was the first of the four Gospels to be written. Rather surprisingly, nowhere in the Gospel is Mark identified as the writer but from very early days he has been regarded as such, and the tradition is so clear and convincing that very few scholars challenge its authenticity. Part of the tradition affirms that Mark was the protégé of Peter and that he wrote down Peter's recollections – including some of his preaching material – to produce a brief life of Jesus which would persuade Gentiles of our Lord's saviourhood. There is evidence enough in the Gospel itself to support the view that Peter was a major source for Mark; although there is evidence that Mark had access to other material also.

Attempts to discover who Mark was have produced a great deal of fascinating speculation. The evidence concerning Mark's identity, and those events and themes which confirm Peter's place in his Gospel, have already been dealt with (*WoL Advent 1992*). But we look with fresh eyes and renewed interest at this man who was so favoured by birth, faith, and circumstance that it was reasonable for him to write the first Gospel.

Many scholars assume that Mark was the young man who escaped capture at Gethsemane when Jesus was taken prisoner (*14:51,52*). If this were not Mark there would be no point in the story being told. He was the son of a certain Mary who was a follower of Jesus to whose house Peter went on his escape from prison (*Acts 12:12*), and it is thought that this was the location of the Upper Room (*14:12–16*). Because he was related to Barnabas (*Col 4:10*) it would be natural for Mark to join Barnabas and Paul on the first missionary journey (*Acts 13:1–5*). Confusingly, in this account he was called John, but many men had two names which were often used singly or together: Mark's full name was John Mark. His evangelistic zeal and connections (*1 Pet 5:13*) fitted him well for his task.

PRAISE
> *You take an ordinary human mind,*
> *Infill it with your Spirit and inspire,*
> *Make knowledge of the Christ a deep desire,*
> *And truth, eternal truth, not hard to find.*
> *Then can all people here and everywhere,*
> *Learn of the Christ and his unwavering care.*

The Beginning of the Gospel
Mark 1:1–3

'The beginning of the gospel about Jesus Christ, the Son of God' (v. 1, NIV).

The straight-from-the-shoulder, all-action style of Peter is apparent from the very first verse of Mark's Gospel. Matthew, the careful gatherer and recorder of information about Jesus, commenced his Gospel with the genealogy of Jesus (*Matt 1:1–17*). Luke chose to start his Gospel in a more literary fashion as befitted an account of the faith being written to a high-status official like Theophilus (*Luke 1:1–4*). It was John who, long after the other Gospels had been written, filled in the missing eternal element of a Christ – the divine Word – he who had been with God from the beginning (*John 1:1,2*). We can almost hear Peter's voice in Mark's statement of the divinity of Jesus and in his reference to Isaiah the prophet introducing us to John the Baptist (*v. 2*). It was Malachi, in fact, the last prophet in the Old Testament, who made the 'messenger' statement (*v. 2b; cf. Mal 3:1*), and Isaiah who spoke of the one who would 'prepare the way for the Lord' (*v. 3; cf. Isa 40:3*).

It is not too difficult to read Mark's Gospel at one sitting and of the many impressions this creates, one of them is energy. Things happened because the Spirit-filled Son of God had come to earth, and no one communicated the energy of the Spirit more powerfully than Peter. The energetic Peter had become the natural leader of the disciple group and his lifestyle and brand of evangelism had influenced Mark powerfully.

We take note of the fact that although this written record is described as Mark's Gospel, Mark was careful to make it clear that he was writing about the gospel of Jesus Christ. The Gospels are the documents, the gospel is the message Jesus proclaimed and embodied. The word gospel means 'good news', and what glorious news it is! Men and women need no longer fear the consequences of their evil ways because the Christ has come to redeem all who would be saved.

PRAISE   *The gospel is good news for all mankind,*
      Because we learn the truths we need to know,
   That pardon, peace and power we might find,
      And through our much-flawed lives God's love can show.
   We merit only judgment and despair –
   But this good news confirms a Father's care.

The Forerunner Arrives
Mark 1:4–8

'And so John came, baptising in the desert region and preaching a baptism of repentance for the forgiveness of sins' (v. 4, NIV).

Peter, who stands behind Mark's Gospel, engaged himself in no detailed description of John the Baptist beyond mentioning his clothing and diet (*v. 6*). These omissions (*cf. Luke 1:5–25,57–80*) would not be due to a lack of regard on Peter's part because he had been – so it is assumed – a disciple of John before becoming a disciple of Jesus (*cf. John 1:35–42*), but Peter always expressed himself in clear and direct terms. It was enough for Peter to make reference to the prophets and then launch into the action.

John the Baptist, an Elijah-like figure whom Jesus described as being the greatest man ever to have been born up to that time (*Matt 11:7–15*), a man prepared from birth to be the forerunner of Christ, came baptising in the desert region. John had chosen for his ministry that part of the Jordan River which ran through the desert area – a wise choice indeed. The desert has often symbolised the spiritual wastelands of the human heart, and the parched, barren earth would match the unfruitful, frustrated lives of many who gathered to hear Israel's first prophet since Malachi.

The crowds who gathered (*v. 5*) received little comfort from John. They were sinful people who needed to repent; that is to say, they needed to change the direction of their lives, and John told them in words impossible for them to misunderstand. In W.E. Vine's definition, this change 'involves both a turning from sin and a turning to God'. The desert places within them could blossom again (*cf. Isa 35:1*). On their repentance – that is, their sorrow for sin and willingness to change – God's forgiveness would follow. That was the good news. The love of God is for all: anyone who is serious about repentance will be forgiven. As another John was later to write, 'If we confess our sins, he is faithful and just and will forgive us our sins and purify us from all unrighteousness' (*1 John 1:9*).

PRAYER

> *Out of my darkness he called me,*
> *Out of my doubt, my despair,*
> *Out of the wastes of my winter,*
> *Into the spring of his care.*

(John Gowans, SASB 378)

Faith that Endures

Luke 18:1–8 (following 20.8.2000)

'However, when the Son of Man comes, will he find faith on the earth?'
(v. 8b, NIV)

From the contrast between the unjust judge who responded to the widow's claims for justice because she was becoming a nuisance (*v. 5*), and our heavenly Father whose actions are governed by a heart of love and righteousness (*v. 7*), Jesus moved to a question related to his second coming. If the question in our key verse seems to be a little unrelated to the parable of the unjust judge, we need to remember that the parable was given at the end of a discourse on the coming of the kingdom of God (*17:20–37*). The subjects of prayer, human injustice, persistence, divine justice, faith and God's willingness to answer prayer are strongly related to the expectation that Jesus will return to our world again. In the model prayer which Jesus gave did he not teach us to pray for the coming of his kingdom (*11:1–4*)? It is with varying degrees of longing that Christ's people look forward to his return in triumph and glory.

Jesus knows the weaknesses within the human soul: its ability to become absorbed with trivial issues and lose sight of the main goals of life, hence the question, 'will he find faith on the earth?' If he came today he would find that in many countries faith is strong and growing stronger. Sadly, however, he would find in other countries that God's people are battling hard, and not always with great success, against the forces of unrighteousness. The arrogance of evil and its pervasiveness are incredible. Will he find faith? In those who ask important questions such as, 'What is the meaning of life?' 'Why do I hunger after a better way?' 'Why do I feel that love should prevail?' faith can be born. When Jesus comes, therefore, he *will* find faith, the quality of which is related to the persistent prayers of his people. Clearly, we have our part to play.

PRAYER

O Lord, let me your own faith share,
Let me, like you, be powerful in prayer,
Let my dull heart begin to yearn
For that blest day when you return.
Now, use my faithful, prayerful heart and mind
To help increase the faith you hope to find.

PRAYER SUBJECT   *For more adventures in evangelism.*

A Better Baptism

Mark 1: 4–8

'I baptise you with water, but he will baptise you with the Holy Spirit' (v. 8, NIV).

The humility of John the Baptist was both natural and attractive. Not at any time did he overreach himself or seek to bring glory to his own name. He was the forerunner – as such he was important – but the one whose coming he heralded was of far greater importance. As John rightly said, 'After me will come one more powerful than I, the thongs of whose sandals I am not worthy to stoop down and untie' (v. 7). Perhaps one of the reasons why God ordained that John should spend his time in the desert areas as he prepared for his life's work, was to keep him unspoiled. Had he been brought up in the city he would have seen too many status-driven priests and posturing Pharisees for his soul's good. There was a shortage of role models in Jerusalem for forerunners of the Messiah.

John was not playing down the significance of his water baptism but he knew, presumably because the Holy Spirit had made it clear to him, that the Messiah's baptism was much more meaningful. When *he* came, he would baptise with the Holy Spirit (v. 8b), a baptism which far exceeded in value the purely symbolic water baptism of John. Scholars point out that John's knowledge of the Holy Spirit was related to the Old Testament and could not, therefore, equal the post-Pentecostal knowledge of the New Testament. Even so, he would be aware of the enormous potential of such a baptism. The way of all genuine prophets had been to make prophecies which were larger than they knew at the time, and this was so with John the Baptist. He knew that the Messiah's baptism would be great, but had no idea just how great it would be. In a sense, the same is true today. The baptism of the Spirit is far greater than any of us can imagine. It is a baptism we value enormously, and the Spirit's liberty, empowering and assurances we know, but its potential in our own lives and in the lives of others is beyond our understanding and will to experience.

PRAYER
Come, thou Witness of his dying;
Come, remembrancer divine!
Let us feel thy power, applying
Christ to every soul, and mine.

(*Charles Wesley, SASB 191*)

The Lord's Baptism (1)
Mark 1:9–11

'At that time Jesus came from Nazareth in Galilee and was baptised by John in the Jordan' (v. 9, NIV).

'At that time' (*v. 9a*) parallels 'And so John came' (*v. 4a*) and reveals the direct, clear and factual approach of Peter who, we recall, is the major source behind Mark's Gospel. Throughout Mark's Gospel we will be struck by the same purposeful, vigorous style, and the record is none the worse for that. At the appointed moment John came from his desert dwelling, and at his appointed time Jesus came from Nazareth. Unlike the other Gospel writers Mark does not go into a great deal of detail about John or the Lord's baptism (*cf. Matt 3:1ff.: Luke 3:1–23, WoL 10,12 June 2000; John 1:6–34*), but that does not mean that the writer, in following his source, Peter, was unimpressed by the event.

Peter saw in our Lord's baptism the beginning of the gospel. He made this clear after the resurrection as the disciples congregated in the Upper Room and it was thought necessary to replace Judas. When he introduced the subject Peter said, '*beginning from John's baptism* to the time when Jesus was taken up from us' (*Acts 1:22*). Later, when Peter was challenged about giving Gentiles entrance to the Christian faith, he said to Cornelius and his household, 'You know what has happened throughout Judea, *beginning in Galilee after the baptism that John preached* – how God anointed Jesus of Nazareth with the Holy Spirit and power' (*Acts 10: 37,38*). Clearly, Peter took a high view of our Lord's baptism by John.

Because of our Lord's sinlessness, his baptism by John was not a baptism of repentance; rather, it was the moment when Jesus was publicly anointed by the Spirit as the Messiah. Our Lord must have had a deepening awareness of his divine nature and role, but the voice of the Father confirmed it with the dramatic and gracious words, 'You are my Son, whom I love; with you I am well pleased' (*v. 11*).

PRAISE
*Christ, when for us you were baptised
God's Spirit on you came,
As peaceful as a dove, and yet
As urgent as a flame.*

(*F. Bland Tucker*)

The Lord's Baptism (2)
Mark 1:9–11

'At that time Jesus came from Nazareth in Galilee and was baptised by John in the Jordan' (v. 9, NIV).

Although Mark's account of our Lord's baptism is brief it ought not to be lightly read. We note, for instance, that as Jesus came out of the water, 'he saw heaven being *torn* open' (*v. 10a*) – there is energy in that word. It is the same word that is used in that moment when Jesus died and the veil of the temple, that barrier which stood between the people and the Holy of Holies in the temple, 'was torn in two from top to bottom' (*Matt 27:51a*). At the beginning of our Lord's earthly ministry and at its conclusion, the eternal world opened, at the first to him, at the second to us all.

Another feature of the baptism of Jesus concerns the Trinity, because God the Father, God and the Son and God the Holy Spirit are identified for us. The concept of three persons in the Godhead is difficult for us to grasp but the facts both of Scripture and experience compel belief in the doctrine. God as Creator and Father we can accept, and we have to accept the divinity of Jesus, because no other explanation does justice to his person and role. What God the Father and God the Son taught us about the Holy Spirit (*cf. John 14:16; Rom 8:9*) convinces us that he, too, is divine. Hard though the doctrine is to explain, it squares with the facts.

Although we have said that our Lord's deepening awareness of his nature and role was confirmed at his baptism (*WoL 29 Aug 2000*), we are not suggesting that he became the Son of God at that time. He was always the Son of God. Mark made that clear when he wrote, 'The beginning of the gospel about Jesus Christ, the Son of God' (*v. 1*). Christ's voluntarily assumed humanity, with all its restrictions, may have clouded the issue, but all became clear at his baptism by John.

PRAISE

He left his Father's throne above,
So free, so infinite his grace,
Emptied himself of all but love
And bled for Adam's helpless race.
'Tis mercy all, immense and free,
For, O my God, it found out me.

(Charles Wesley, SASB 283)

A Time of Testing
Mark 1:12,13

'At once the Spirit sent him out into the desert' (v. 12, NIV).

From the glory of Jordan, the opening of heaven, the baptism by the Spirit and the voice of the Father confirming his Sonship, Jesus was sent by the Spirit into the desert. Our version (*NIV*) conceals the force of the original Greek behind the word 'sent'; some translations say the Spirit 'drove him' (*NKJV, REB, JM*) and another says 'impelled' (*NASB*). Matthew and Luke use more gentle language simply saying that Jesus was 'led by the Spirit' (*Matt 4:1; Luke 4:1*). There would be no question concerning our Lord's obedience to the Spirit's direction, but Christ's mission was commenced in the disciplined, purposeful way it was to continue.

If Jesus needed time for thought, to establish his priorities and method of working, the desert would be an ideal place and, for good measure, Satan was there to apply his devious and discerning pressures (*v. 2; Matt 4:1–11*). Our Lord's victory over temptation and extended period in the desert was, for him, an essential time of testing. Victory there meant that he had proved himself for the even more demanding days ahead. His victory has meaning for us also: because he triumphed we too can triumph. If he could move from the heights of exultation to the troughs of hardship and temptation and be stronger for it then we, who have been filled with his Spirit, can be positive about our personal experiences of the desert.

Although Mark's account of our Lord's period in the desert is brief, his comments have stimulated the imagination of scholars through the years. Some, for instance, see in the reference to wild animals (*v. 13b*) not so much an indication of the desert's desolation, as the fulfilment of the prophecy that with the Messiah wild animals can live at peace with each other (*cf. Job 5:22,23; Isa 11:6–8*). The ministering angels (*v. 13*) convey the truth that even in the most desolate of situations God has those who work well on his behalf.

PRAYER

> When I'm tempted to do wrong,
> Make me steadfast, wise and strong;
> And when all alone I stand,
> Shield me with thy mighty hand.

(*John Page Hopps, SASB*

INDEX

(as from: January 1995)

...d Scripture passages are used for the extended coverage given to
...reat Christian festivals from which each separate volume takes
...days and the New Year are also given separate treatment, too
...cluded in a general index.